sona
BOOKS

**First published in the UK 2023 by Sona Books
an imprint of Danann Media Publishing Ltd.**

© 2023 Danann Media Publishing Limited

Proofreader: Finn O'Neill

© 2023 Future Publishing PLC

CAT NO: **SON0578**
ISBN: **978-1-915343-39-0**

Made in EU.

Crochet Toy Box

Create toys & games the family will love

WELCOME

Every kid loves to have fun – so why not fill up their
toybox with delightful handmade toys?
From bears and dolls to rattles and lovies, we've got
everything you need to create crochet toys and games
for the little ones in your life. They can take a trip to
Mexico with an amigurumi doll, learn colours and shapes
with fun geometric patterns, and battle each other in
naughts and crosses.
For crochet beginners, we've also included a handy
guide to get you started in the craft. So what are you
waiting for? You're just a stitch away…

CONTENTS

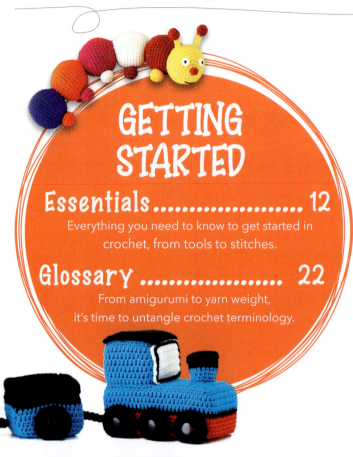

GETTING STARTED

Essentials 12

Everything you need to know to get started in crochet, from tools to stitches.

Glossary 22

From amigurumi to yarn weight, it's time to untangle crochet terminology.

Animals

Baby

Dolls & Bears

Toys

Games

GETTING STARTED

The essentials

LEARN THE BASICS TO GET YOU STARTED ON YOUR CROCHETING JOURNEY

HOLDING YOUR HOOK

OVERHAND (KNIFE GRIP)

This technique is also known as the knife grip, as you grip the crochet hook as if you're holding a knife. Place your hand over the hook, then support the handle in your chosen palm.

UNDERHAND (PENCIL GRIP)

For this technique, hold the hook like a pencil (hence the name pencil grip). Hold the thumb rest between your thumb and index finger and then let the handle rest on top of your hand.

HOLDING YOUR YARN

THE LOOSE-YARN HOLD

Holding the end of the yarn in your right hand and with your left palm facing you, weave the yarn in front of your little finger, behind your ring finger, in front of your middle finger and behind your index finger.

THE PINKY HOLD

Looping the yarn once around your little finger may help you to keep a secure grip. Follow the instructions for the loose-yarn hold, but begin by looping the yarn around your little finger clockwise.

MAKE A SLIPKNOT

MAKE A LOOP

Wrap the yarn once around two of your fingers on your left hand to form a loop, making sure to leave a tail of at least 10cm (or longer if your pattern calls for it).

DRAW UP A LOOP

Take the loop off the hook and grip between your thumb and fingers. Insert your hook from right to left, catch the working yarn and pull through to make a loop on your hook.

PULL TO CLOSE THE LOOP

Grip the tail and the working yarn and pull them tight to form a knot. Pull the working yarn to tighten the loop around your hook. It needs to be able to move up and down your hook so don't pull too tight.

CHAIN STITCH (CH)

YARN OVER & DRAW UP LOOP

Starting with a slipknot, move your hook underneath your yarn and pull this through the loop already on your hook.

KEEP GOING

Keep going to create a chain of the length needed in your pattern. Try not to make the stitches too tight as this will make it difficult when working subsequent rows. Keep the stitches even or you will get an uneven edge on your piece.

COUNTING CHAINS

To count the chains, identify the Vs on the side that's facing you. Each of these is one chain. The V above the slipknot is your first chain, but don't count the loop on your hook. This is the working loop and does not count as a chain. If you are creating a very long chain , it might help to mark every 10 or 20 stitches with a stitch marker.

SLIPSTICH (SS/SL ST)

INTO CHAIN

Insert your hook into the second chain from the hook. Yarn over (yo). Pull your hook back through the chain. There should be two loops on your hook.

PULL THROUGH

Avoiding the urge to yarn over, continue to pull the yarn through the second loop on the hook. You have completed the stitch and should have one loop on your hook.

LEFT HANDED?

All the tutorials in this book can be followed by left-handed crocheters. Simply reverse the instructions and hold the picture tutorials up to a mirror to see how you should be working. So every time you see 'Right' replace it with 'Left' and every time you see 'Clockwise' replace with 'Counterclockwise' (and vice versa)

WORKING THE FOUNDATION CHAIN

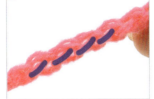

FRONT OF THE CHAIN

Looking at the front side of your chain, you will see a row of sideways Vs, each with two loops - a top loop and a bottom loop.

BACK OF THE CHAIN

When you look at the back side of the chain, you will see a line of bumps in between the loops. These are called the back bumps.

It doesn't matter which method you use as long as you are consistent when moving along the chain. Working under the top loop is the easiest method for beginners, but does not create as neat an edge as working under the back bumps.

METHOD 1: TOP LOOP

For this method, hook under the top loop only.

METHOD 2: TOP TWO LOOPS

Hooking under both the top loop and the back bump is sometimes referred to as the top two loops of the chain.

METHOD 3: TOP LOOP AND BACK BUMP

Turn over your chain so that the back bumps are facing you. Insert your hook under the back bump.

UK and US terms

Confusingly, patterns can follow either UK or US naming conventions. To make things even more difficult, the same name is used to mean different stitches under either convention.

Most patterns will state whether they are using US or UK terminology, but if not, checking the pattern's country of origin may be a good place to start.

A handy trick to remember is that there is no stitch called a single crochet (sc) in UK terminology, so if you see this on the pattern, then you know it is using US naming conventions.

UK	US
Chain (ch)	Chain (ch)
Double crochet (dc)	Single crochet (sc)
Treble crochet (tr)	Double crochet (dc)
Half treble crochet (htr)	Half double crochet (hdc)
Double treble crochet (dtr)	Triple (treble) crochet (tr)
Slip stitch (sl st/ss)	Slip stitch (sl st/ss)

Crochet TOYBOX

DOUBLE CROCHET (DC)

INSERT HOOK
Working into your foundation chain, find the second chain from your hook and insert your hook.

DRAW UP A LOOP
Yarn over (yo), then draw up a loop. You will now have two loops on your crochet hook.

PULL TO CLOSE THE LOOP
Yarn over and then draw the yarn through both loops on the hook so you have one loop left on your hook. You have now completed the stitch.

TREBLE CROCHET (TR)

INSERT HOOK
Working into your foundation chain, identify the fourth chain from your hook. Make a yarn over (yo) and then insert your hook into the fourth chain from the hook.

YARN OVER AND DRAW UP A LOOP
Yarn over, then draw up a loop. There should now be three loops on your hook.

YARN OVER AND DRAW UP A LOOP
Yarn over, then draw the yarn through two of the loops on your hook. There should now be two loops on your hook.

COMPLETE THE STITCH
Yarn over and then draw the yarn through the two loops left on the hook. You have completed the stitch and should have one loop on your hook.

DOUBLE TREBLE CROCHET (DTR)

MAKE A LOOP
Working into your foundation chain, identify the fifth chain from your hook. Yarn over twice and insert your hook into the fifth chain from the hook. Yarn over and draw up a loop. There should be four loops on your hook. Yarn over, then draw the yarn through two of the loops on your hook. There should now be three loops on your hook.

DRAW UP A LOOP
Yarn over, then draw the yarn through two of the loops on your hook again. There should now be two loops on your hook. Yarn over, then draw the yarn through the two loops on your hook. There should now be one loop on your hook. You have completed the stitch.

HALF TREBLE CROCHET (HTR)

INSERT HOOK
Working into your foundation chain, identify the third chain from your hook. Make a yarn over (yo) and then insert your hook into the third chain from the hook.

YARN OVER AND DRAW UP A LOOP
Yarn over, then draw up a loop. There should now be three loops on your hook. Yarn over, then draw the yarn through all three loops on your hook. The stitch is now complete and there should be one loop on your hook.

IDENTIFYING STITCHES

There are two ways to count stitches: either by counting the Vs along the top of the work or by counting the posts. If you count the Vs, make sure you never count the loop that is on your hook. When counting either Vs or posts, you must take careful consideration when you come to the turning chain. If it is counted as a stitch in your pattern, then count it, but if not, leave it out.

Turning chain

WORKING ROWS

UNDER BOTH

Hooking under the front and back loops of the stitch is the most common way to work into a row. Use this method unless told otherwise.

INSERT YOUR HOOK

After the turning chain, insert your hook so that it goes in under both the front and back loops of the V.

FRONT AND BACK LOOPS ONLY (FLO AND BLO)

Sometimes a pattern will say to work into Front or Back loops only. Doing so will create ridges in your work, for example, you may use FLO/BLO to add ribbing to a hat. To work into Front loops only (FLO) identify the loop closest to you and work into the stitch as normal. For Back loops, use the loop farthest away from you.

JOIN A NEW YARN

THE LAST STITCH

When you think you don't have enough yarn left in your current ball, or you need to change colour, begin the last stitch of your current row with the old yarn, but stop before you reach the final step (yo and draw through all loops on hook).

DRAW UP A LOOP

Make a yarn over (yo) with the new ball of yarn and complete the stitch. Leave a tail of at least a 15cm (5.9in) on the new yarn. Continue crocheting with the new yarn, and drop the old yarn. You can hide the ends in the inside of your project.

CHANGING COLOUR

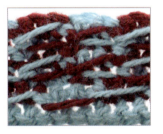

ALONG THE EDGE

When you're creating stripes by changing colour at the beginning of every row or so, you can leave the unworked yarn dangling at the edge. This way you can pick it up again when you need to. To do this, carry it loosely up the edge of the work in order to begin your new row. Adding an edge or border will hide the carried yarn strands.

OVER THE TOP OF THE OLD YARN

If you need to change colours regularly and mid-row, crocheting over the top of the yarn you're not currently using is a good way to keep it concealed and eliminates ends that would need weaving in. This technique is great when you are creating a reversible fabric, as it keeps both sides looking neat.

FLOATING STRANDS

If only one side of your final product will be seen, then you can carry the unused colours along the back of the work. Just drop the yarn you're not using, then pick it up again when you need it, loosely bringing it across the back of the work. This works best if the strands are only a few stitches long. If they are longer, cut the threads and weave in instead.

CUTTING THE YARN

If you are putting in a big block of one colour, it's best to cut the yarn and treat it like you're joining a new yarn, then weave in the ends of the yarn at a later stage.

Crochet TOYBOX

Turning chains

Whenever you turn your work, you will need to create a turning chain to start your next row. When using anything but double crochet, the turning chain always counts as the first stitch (unless specified otherwise), and the next stitch should be created in the second stitch from the hook. Different stitches need different heights of turning chains, to match the height of the stitch about to be made.

Stitch (UK)	Number of turning chains (t-ch)
Double crochet (dc)	1
Half-treble crochet (htr)	2
Treble crochet (tr)	3
Double treble crochet (dtr)	4

INCREASE

INCREASING IN THE MIDDLE OF A ROW (TREBLES AS EXAMPLE)

Make a treble crochet in the next stitch. Make another treble crochet in the same stitch. You have increased your stitch count by one.

INCREASING AT THE START OF A ROW

As the turning chain normally counts as a stitch (except in dc), increasing at the start of a row is different. To increase, insert your hook into the first stitch at the base of the chain and make the stitch. The stitch you've just made and the turning chain count as two stitches, and you have made an increase.

DECREASE

DOUBLE CROCHET TWO STITCHES TOGETHER (DC2TOG)

Insert your hook into the next stitch, as if to make a double crochet. Draw up a loop. Without completing the stitch, insert your hook into the next stitch as if to make another double crochet. Draw up a loop. You should now have three loops on your hook. Yarn over (yo) and draw the loop through all three stitches on your hook. Having worked into two stitches, but only created one, you have decreased by one.

TREBLE CROCHET THREE STITCHES TOGETHER

(TR3TOG) Yarn over and insert your hook into the next stitch, as if to make a treble crochet. Draw up a loop, yarn over and draw through two loops on the hook. There should now be two loops on your hook. *Without completing the stitch, yarn over and insert your hook into the next stitch. Draw up a loop, yarn over and draw through two loops on the hook.* There should now be three loops on your hook. Repeat * to * into the next stitch. There should now be four loops on your hook, yarn over and draw the yarn through all four loops to complete the decrease.

STARTING IN THE ROUND

METHOD 1: SINGLE CHAIN START

Chain two. Now make a double crochet (dc) into the second chain from your hook. Make the rest of your doubles into the same chain stitch as your first double crochet.

METHOD 2: MULTIPLE CHAIN START

Make a short chain, depending on the pattern that you're following. Here we have shown five chains. Create a slip stitch (sl st) into the first chain that you created. Work your first round into the middle of the ring you have just made. Now either continue to work in a spiral or connect the last double crochet to the first with a slip stitch, create your turning chains and continue.

METHOD 3: MAGIC RING (MR)

Also called a magic circle (mc). To begin, create a loop (as if to create a slipknot), hold the yarn where the loop crosses over, with the starting tail in front, and insert your hook from front to back.

■ Yarn over with the working yarn and pull up a loop back through to the front. Yarn over your hook again, this time from above the loop, and pull through to create a chain on your ring.

■ To create your first dc, insert your hook into the ring, with both the loop and starting tail above your hook. Your stitches will now be created around both yarns. Yarn over and draw up a loop back to the front of the ring. Create your stitch as you would usually. Carry on until you have the number of stitches you need.

■ Once you have created all of your stitches, keep your hook in the loop and hold it and your round in your dominant hand. Pull on the starting tail to close the gap.

Turned

Not turned

WORKING IN THE ROUND

CONTINUOUS SPIRAL

To start each new round, work the first stitch into the top of the first stitch of the last round. Now add your stitch marker into this stitch by slipping it through the loops. Now continue to stitch the rest of your round as stated in the pattern until you reach the stitch before the marker. This is the last stitch of the round.

To start your next round, remove the marker, crochet the stitch as normal and then replace the marker into the stitch you have just created.

When finishing your spiral you will need to smooth out the jump in stitches between rows. To do so, slip stitch into the next stitch. For taller stitches, gradually crochet shorter stitches i.e if you have used tr stitches you will end with a htr, dc, ss.

JOINED ROUNDS

Alternatively you can add a ss at the end of each row which gives the appearance of concentric circles rather than a spiral. If you do this, to create your next round, create a chain to the height of your stitch. One for double, two for half treble, three for treble and so on.

TURN YOUR WORK

When you create your next rows you have the choice of turning your work or continuing on around the circle (the same as a spiral stitch). Alternatively, you can turn your work at the end of each round, and it will create a slightly different look. After turning your work, you will continue to work each of the rounds the same way.

FASTENING OFF

SECURE YOUR WORK

When you've finished your project, cut the working yarn about 15cm (6in) from the last stitch (or longer if your pattern states). Yarn over (yo) with the tail. Pull the yarn through the loop on your hook, and keep pulling until the cut end goes through the loop. Grab the tail and pull it tight, to close the last loop. Your stitches are now secure.

FIXING MISTAKES

UNDO YOUR WORK

When you notice that things have gone awry, take your hook out of the working loop and grab hold of the working yarn. Pull on the working yarn to unravel the stitches one by one. This process is also known as frogging. Keep pulling the working yarn until you've unravelled the mistake, then simply insert your hook into the working loop and begin redoing the work you've just undone, but this time without the mistake!

JOINING

METHOD 1: WHIP STITCH

Hold two pieces together with the wrong sides facing each other. Pass your needle through the V stitches on both pieces from front to back and pull the yarn through. Draw your needle back to the front and repeat. Using a whip stitch will leave a visible line on both sides of the piece. This won't be quite as obvious when you are using the same colour.

METHOD 2: MATTRESS STITCH

Lay your pieces side-by-side with the right sides facing you. Leaving a 15cm tail, insert your needle into the first edge stitch of the first piece and then down through the edge of the second. Insert your needle down through the first stitch of piece one and up through to the second stitch. Now repeat on piece two. Keep going and a loose 'ladder' will start to form. When you have done about 2.5cm, pull gently on the yarn to draw the two sides together. Repeat until you have reached the end, the seam will be almost invisible.

METHOD 3: SLIP STITCH OR DOUBLE CROCHET

Insert your hook through the first stitch on both pieces. Complete a slip stitch (or double crochet) and repeat, ensuring you match up the stitches as you go.

■ A slip stitch seam is strong, and will be almost invisible from the other side of the work. Slip stitches do not allow for any give, so making them too tight will pucker the fabric.

■ Using a double crochet will give a more pronounced edge, giving a more decorative seam. It is also stretchier than a slip stitch join.

METHOD 4: FLAT SLIP-STITCHED SEAM

Insert your hook from top to bottom through the back loop only on the right-hand piece of fabric. Do the same on your left piece, then yarn over (yo) and pull through both loops on the hook. Repeat until you reach the end. This seam produces a flat row of chain-looking stitches. It's a neat finish and adds a nice little detail to your seams.

To join amigurumi it is helpful to pin your pieces in place. Join using one of the methods above, inserting your needle from bottom to top of the piece you are attaching. Pull tight on the yarn for a seamless join.

YARN WEIGHTS

Yarn weight	Properties	Ideal for...
Lace, 2-ply, fingering	Extremely light, Lace yarn produces a very delicate texture on a 2mm (US 0) hook. Bigger hooks will produce a more open fabric.	Lace
Superfine, 3-ply, fingering, baby	Using a very slim hook, Superfine yarn is perfect for lightweight, intricate lace work.	Finely woven socks, shawls, babywear
Fine, 4-ply, sport, baby	Fine yarn is great for socks, and can also be used in items that feature slightly more delicate textures.	Light jumpers, babywear, socks, accessories
Double knit (DK), light worsted, 5/6-ply	An extremely versatile weight yarn, DK can be used to create a wide variety of items and crochets up relatively quickly.	Jumpers, light-weight scarves, blankets, toys
Aran, medium worsted, Afghan, 12-ply	With many yarns in this thickness using a variety of fibres to make them machine washable, Aran yarn is good for garments with thick cabled detail and functional items.	Jumpers, cabled garments, blankets, hats, scarves, mittens
Chunky, bulky, craft, rug, 14-ply	Quick to crochet, chunky yarn is perfect for warm outerwear. Often made from lightweight fibres to prevent drooping.	Rugs, jackets, blankets, hats, legwarmers, winter accessories
Super chunky, super bulky, bulky, roving, 16-ply and upwards	Commonly used with very large hooks, Super chunky yarn crochets up very quickly. Large stitches make mistakes easy to spot.	Heavy blankets, rugs, thick scarves

HOOK SIZE
CONVERSION TABLE

UK Size	US Size
2mm, 2.25mm	B/1
2.5mm, 2.75mm	C/2
3mm, 3.25mm	D/3
3.5mm	E/4
3.75mm, 4mm	F/5
4mm, 4.25mm	G/6
4.5mm	G/7
5mm	H/8
5.5mm	I/9
6mm	J/10
6.5mm, 7mm	K/10.5
8mm	L/11
9mm	M/13
10mm	N,P/15

WHICH HOOK?

Every ball of yarn comes with a recommended hook size, which is printed on the label. Use bigger hooks than this to make a more open stitch, and smaller ones to make a tighter, more compact fabric. We suggest using a smaller hook than recommended for amigurumi projects.

TENSION

Tension or gauge is the measure of how many stitches and rows you need to create a specific length and width of crocheted fabric. The size of your hook, weight of your yarn and your own tension while crocheting will all have an effect on any piece that you're creating. If you naturally crochet very tight or loose stitches, then the final product dimensions will be different to those provided in a pattern. Tension square patterns will sometimes be given with your pattern and allow you to work out how tight to make your stitches before you start. Usually these will be 10cm square.

When making things like children's toys or blankets, there is a bit more freedom when following a pattern. However, when creating garments to exact fitted measurements, tension squares are incredibly important.

With amigurumi a loose tension will show the stuffing between the stitches. It's difficult to be too tight with amigurumi, however you should still be able to work stitches reasonably easily. If needed, switch to a smaller hook for a neater finish.

Amigurumi
Tension too
loose

Amigurumi
correct tension

BLOCKING

Blocking is a process you will use after making many of your flat projects. It sets the stitches in place, adds definition to lace pieces and strengthens any straight edges in your work.

PIN YOUR WORK

No matter which method you choose to use, you will need to pin the corners to the correct measurement for your final piece.

Next pin half way along the edge, and keep doing this until you are happy that the edges are all straight and even. If you are blocking any crocheted segments that are due to be joined, make sure you measure them out so they match when you come to sew them together.

For more refined edging, thread a blocking wire through each of the stitches or row ends along the straight edge of your project.

METHOD 1: SPRAY BLOCKING

Spray blocking is the easiest and quickest way of blocking your work. Pin and then take a spray bottle and give a few sprays of water until the surface of your work is evenly saturated. Gently pat the surface to help the water absorb into the yarn fibres. Leave your work to dry; this can sometimes take over 24 hours.

METHOD 2: STEAM BLOCKING

This method requires an iron or handheld steamer. Do not touch the iron to the yarn at any point. Man-made fibres will melt, and all your work and your iron will be damaged. Pin your work then hold an iron about 2.5cm (1in) from the surface of your project. Steam until the entire surface area is moist to the touch. Once done, pat the surface gently with your hands and leave to dry.

METHOD 3: WET BLOCKING (BEST FOR LACE WORK)

Fill your sink or bath with lukewarm water. You can add in no-rinse wool wash if you wish. Immerse your project in the water, until saturated. Leave it for 20 minutes then take your project out and gently squeeze out the excess liquid. Do not wring your project, as this will stretch it out of shape. Continue until you can remove no more water. Lay a towel on a flat surface and lie your garment flat. Gently roll up your towel to press out even more water. Pin your project to your blocking surface (a foam mat or mattress is ideal) and leave to dry. If working on a straight-edged lace garment you will need to use a lot of pins and/or blocking wire along the edge of to obtain a professional result. The edge will bow if you don't use enough pins and spoil the finish.

ADDITIONAL USEFUL TERMS

ASTERISK* /BRACKETS( )

A symbol used to mark a point in a pattern row, usually at the beginning of a set of repeated instructions.

CHART/STITCH DIAGRAM

A visual depiction of a crochet pattern that uses symbols to represent stitches.

CROSSED STITCHES

Two or more tall stitches that are crossed, one in front of the other, to create an X shape.

FIBREFILL

Toy stuffing used to stuff amigurumi projects.

LINKED STITCH

A variation of any standard tall stitch that links the stitch to its neighbour partway up the post to eliminate the gaps between stitches and form a solid fabric.

POST

The vertical stem of a stitch.

POST STITCH

A stitch formed by crocheting around the post of the stitch in the row or round below, so the stitch sits in front of (or behind) the surface of the fabric.

RIGHT SIDE (RS)

The side of a crocheted piece that's visible when finished.

ROUND (RND)

A line of stitches worked around a circular crocheted piece.

ROW

A line of stitches worked across a flat crocheted piece.

SPACE (SP)

A gap formed between or beneath stitches, often seen in lace patterns.

STITCH MARKER

A small tool you can slide into a crochet stitch to mark a position. You can use a scrap of yarn or a hairgrip instead.

TAIL

A short length of unworked yarn left at the start or end of a piece.

V

The two loops at the top of each stitch that from a sideways V shape; standard crochet stitches are worked into both these loops.

WEAVE IN

A method used to secure and hide the yarn tails by stitching them through your crocheted stitches.

WORKING LOOP

The single loop that remains on your hook after completing a crochet stitch.

WRONG SIDE (WS)

The side of a crocheted piece that will be hidden; the inside or back.

YARN WEIGHT

The thickness of the yarn (not the weight of a ball of yarn).

ABBREVIATIONS AND SYMBOLS

UK stitch name	Abbreviation	Symbol	Description
back loop	BL		The loop furthest from you at the top of the stitch.
back post double crochet	BPdc		Yarn over, insert the hook from the back to the front, then to the back around the post of the next stitch, yarn over and draw up a loop, (yarn over and draw through two loops) twice.
chain(s)	ch(s)		Yarn over and draw through the loop on the hook.
chain space(s)	ch-sp(s)		The space beneath one or more chains.
double crochet	dc	X or +	Insert the hook into the next stitch and draw up a loop, yarn over and draw through both loops on the hook.
double crochet 2 together	dc2tog		(Insert the hook into the next stitch and draw up a loop) twice, yarn over and draw through all three loops on the hook.
double treble crochet	dtr		Yarn over twice, insert the hook into the next stitch and draw up a loop, (yarn over and draw through two loops on the hook) three times.
front loop	FL		The loop closest to you at the top of the stitch.
front post treble crochet	FPtr		Yarn over, insert the hook from the front to the back to the front around the post of the next stitch, yarn over and draw up a loop, (yarn over and draw through two loops) twice.
half treble crochet	htr		Yarn over, insert the hook into the next stitch and draw up a loop, yarn over and draw through all three loops on the hook.
repeat	rep		Replicate a series of given instructions.
skip	sk		Pass over a stitch or stitches – do not work into it.
slip stitch	ss/sl st	● or ●	Insert the hook into the next stitch, draw up a loop through the stitch and the loop on the hook.
stitch(es)	st(s)		A group of one or more loops of yarn pulled through each other in a specified order until only 1 remains on the hook.
treble crochet	tr		Yarn over, insert the hook into the next stitch and draw up a loop, (yarn over and draw through two loops on the hook) twice.
treble crochet 2 together	tr2tog		Yarn over, insert the hook into the next stitch and draw up a loop, (yarn over and draw through two loops on the hook).
turning chain	t-ch		The chain made at the start of a row to bring your hook and yarn up to the height of the next row.
yarn over	yo		Pass the yarn over the hook so the yarn is caught in the throat of the hook.

If a pattern requires stitches that are not mentioned in this essentials section, stitch instructions will be given on the pattern page.

CROCHET GLOSSARY

AMIGURUMI
The Japanese art of knitting or crocheting small, stuffed yarn creatures.

ASTERISK*
A symbol used to mark a point in a pattern row, usually at the beginning of a set of repeated instructions.

BACK LOOP (BL) ONLY
A method of crocheting in which you work into only the back loop of a stitch instead of both loops.

BACK POST (BP) STITCHES
Textured stitches worked from the back around the post of the stitch below.

BALL BAND
The paper wrapper around a ball of yarn that contains information such as fibre content, amount/length of yarn, weight, colour and dye lot.

BLOCK
A finishing technique that uses moisture to set stitches and shape pieces to their final measurements.

BLOCKING WIRE
A long, straight wire used to hold the edges of crochet pieces straight during blocking, most often for lace.

BOBBLE
A crochet stitch that stands out from the fabric, formed from several incomplete tall stitches joined at the top and bottom.

BRACKETS [ ] OR ( )
Symbols used to surround a set of grouped instructions, often used to indicate repeats.

CHAIN (CH)
The most simple crochet stitch that often forms the foundation that other stitches are worked into.

CHAIN SPACE (CH-SP)
A space in your work that is created by making a chain. The space is located below the chain.

CHAINLESS FOUNDATION
A stretchy foundation plus first row of stitches that are made in one step. Often used in flatwork pieces.

CHAINLESS FOUNDATION STITCHES
Stitches that have an extra chain at the bottom so they can be worked into without first crocheting a foundation chain.

CHART
A visual depiction of a crochet pattern that uses symbols to represent stitches.

CLUSTER
A combination stitch formed from several incomplete tall stitches joined at the top.

CONTRAST COLOUR (CC)
A yarn colour used as an accent to the project's main colour.

CROCHET HOOK
The tool used to form all crochet stitches.

CROSSED STITCHES
Two or more tall stitches that are crossed, one in front of the other, to create an X shape.

Double crochet

Knife grip

DECREASE (DEC)
A shaping technique in which you reduce the number of stitches in your work.

DOUBLE CROCHET
The most basic crochet stitch.

DOUBLE TREBLE CROCHET (DTR)
A basic crochet stitch three times as tall as a double crochet stitch.

DRAPE
The way in which your crocheted fabric hangs; how stiff or flowing it feels.

DRAW UP A LOOP
To pull up a loop of yarn through a stitch or space after inserting your hook into that stitch or space.

FAN
A group of several tall stitches crocheted into the same base stitch and usually separated by chains to form a fan shape.

FASTEN OFF
To lock the final stitch with the yarn end so the crocheted work cannot unravel.

FASTEN ON
To draw up a loop of new yarn through a stitch in preparation to begin crocheting.

FOUNDATION CHAIN
A base chain into which most crochet is worked (unless worked in the round).

FOUNDATION STITCHES, CHAINLESS
See chainless foundation stitches.

FRINGE
A decorative edging made from strands of yarn knotted along the edge.

FROG
To unravel your crochet work by removing your hook and pulling the working yarn. Not the animal.

FRONT LOOP (FL) ONLY
A method in which you work into only the front loop of a stitch instead of both loops.

FRONT POST (FP) STITCHES
Textured stitches worked from the front around the post of the stitch below.

GAUGE (TENSION)
See tension.

HALF TREBLE CROCHET
A basic stitch halfway between the height of a double and treble crochet stitch.

INCREASE (INC)
A shaping technique in which you add extra stitches to your work.

INVISIBLE FINISH
A method of finishing a round or edging so the join is not visible. This requires a yarn needle to finish.

KNIFE GRIP
An overhand method of holding a crochet hook, similar to holding a knife.

Crochet TOYBOX

Treble crochet

Magic ring

Working in the round

Popcorn stitch

LINKED STITCH
A variation of any standard tall stitch that links the stitch to its neighbour partway up the post to eliminate the gaps between stitches and form a solid fabric.

LOOP STITCH
A stitch that creates a loop instead of pulling the stitch through completely.

MAGIC RING
A technique to begin working in the round without leaving a hole in the centre by crocheting over an adjustable loop.

MAIN COLOUR (MC)
The predominant yarn colour of a project.

MATTRESS STITCH
A stitch to sew a seam that forms an almost invisible join on the right side of the work and a ridged seam on the wrong side.

MOTIF
A crocheted shape usually worked in the round as a geometric shape and combined with other motifs into larger pieces.

PARENTHESES ( )
Symbols used in crochet patterns to surround a set of grouped instructions, often used to indicate repeats.

PENCIL GRIP
An underhand method of holding a crochet hook, similar to holding a pencil.

PICOT
A tiny loop of chain stitches that sits on top of a stitch and creates a small shape.

POPCORN
A combination stitch that stands out from the fabric formed from several tall stitches pulled together by a chain stitch.

POST
The main vertical stem of a stitch.

POST STITCH
A stitch formed by crocheting around the post of the stitch in the row or round below, so the stitch sits in front of (or behind) the surface of the fabric.

PUFF STITCH
A combination crochet stitch that forms a smooth, puffy shape created from several incomplete half treble crochet stitches that are joined at the top and bottom.

REPEAT (REP)
To replicate a series of crochet instructions; one instance of the duplicated instructions.

REVERSE DOUBLE CROCHET
A variation of double crochet that is worked backwards (left to right) around the edge of a piece, producing a corded edging.

RIGHT SIDE (RS)
The side of a crocheted piece that's visible.

RIP BACK
To unravel your crochet work.

ROUND (RND)
A line of stitches worked around a circular crocheted piece.

ROW
A line of stitches worked across a flat crocheted piece.

SHELL
A group of several tall stitches, crocheted into the same base stitch, that spread out at the top into a shell shape.

SKIP (SK)
To pass over a stitch or stitches.

SLIP KNOT
A knot that can be tightened by pulling one end of the yarn; used for attaching the yarn to the hook to begin crocheting.

SLIP STITCH (SS OR SL ST)
A stitch with no height, primarily used to join rounds and stitches to move the hook and yarn into a new position.

SPACE (SP)
A gap formed between or beneath stitches, often seen in lace patterns.

SPIKE STICH
A stitch worked around existing stitches to extend down to one or more rows below, creating a long vertical spike.

STITCH (ST)
A group of one or more loops of yarn pulled through each other in a specific order until only one loop remains on the crochet hook.

STITCH DIAGRAM
A map of a crochet or stitch pattern, where each stitch is represented by a symbol.

STITCH MARKER
A small tool you can slide into a stitch or between stitches to mark a position.

SWATCH
A crocheted sample of a stitch pattern large enough to measure the tension (gauge) and test the pattern with a specific hook and yarn.

TAIL
A short length of unworked yarn left at the start or end of a piece.

TENSION (GAUGE)
A measure of how many stitches and rows fit into a certain length of crocheted fabric, usually 10 centimetres (4 inches), that indicates the size of each stitch.

TOGETHER (TOG)
A shaping technique in which you work two or more stitches into one to reduce the number of stitches.

TREBLE CROCHET (TR)
A basic stitch twice as tall as a double crochet.

TURNING CHAIN (T-CH)
A chain made at the start of a row to bring your hook and yarn up to the height of the next row.

V
The two loops at the top of each stitch that form a sideways V shape; standard crochet stitches are worked into both these loops.

V STITCH
A group of two tall stitches crocheted into the same base stitch and separated by one or more chains, forming a V shape.

WEAVE IN
A method used to secure and hide the yarn tails by stitching them through your crocheted stitches.

WHIP STITCH
A simple stitch to sew a seam by inserting the needle through the edge of both crocheted pieces at once to form each stitch.

WORKING IN THE ROUND
Crocheting in a circle instead of back and forward in straight rows, particularly used in amigurumi projects.

WORKING LOOP
The single loop that remains on your hook after completing a crochet stitch.

WRONG SIDE (WS)
The side of a crocheted piece that will be hidden; the inside or back.

YARDAGE
A length of yarn, usually expressed as an estimate of the amount of yarn required for a project.

YARN NEEDLE
A wide, blunt-tipped needle with an eye large enough for the yarn to pass through that's used for stitching crocheted pieces together and weaving in ends.

YARN OVER (YO)
To pass the yarn over the hook so the yarn is caught in the throat of the hook in order to create longer stitches.

YARN TAIL
See tail.

YARN WEIGHT
The thickness of the yarn (not the literal weight of a ball or yarn).

BABY

WITH MUCH LOVE...

BLANKET, BOOTEES AND TOY – GIFTS GALORE FOR
A NEWBORN BABE

You Will Need...

Yarn:
- DK weight yarn in your chosen colours, here we have used 4 x 50g (125m) balls of Rico Design Baby Cotton Soft DK (50% cotton, 50% acrylic) in each of:
- White (001)
- Lobster (029)
- Mint (031)*
- Length of black yarn for embroidery.

Tools:
- 3.5mm hook

Other:
- Washable toy stuffing

BLANKET

MOTIF
(Make 42)
With 3.5mm hook and Mint, ch 21.
ROW 1: 1dc in 2nd ch from hook (counts as 1 st), 1dc in each ch to end, turn(20 sts)
Twisting yarns together on wrong sides when changing colours and working last dc before colour change as follows: with yarn used, insert hook in next dc, yrh and pull through, with next colour, yrh and pull through 2 loops on hook, continue thus:

Pattern

Finished product size: Blanket: Approximately 67 x 77cm/60½ x 30¼in.
Bootees: To fit ages 3-6 months. Toy: 15cm/6in wide and 13cm/5in high
* **TENSION:** 22 stitches and 25 rows, to 10 x 10cm, over double crochet, using 3.50 hook.
* **NOTE:** Yarn amounts are based on average requirements and are therefore approximate. Instructions in square brackets are worked as stated after 2nd bracket.

ROW 2: With Mint, 1ch (does not count as a st throughout), 1dc in each of first 19dc, with White, 1dc in last dc, turn.
ROW 3: With White, 1ch, 1dc in each of first 2dc, with Mint, 1dc in each of last 18dc, turn.
ROW 4: With Mint, 1ch, 1dc in each of first 17dc, with White, 1dc in each of last 3dc, turn.
ROW 5: With White, 1ch, 1dc in each of first 4dc, with Mint, 1dc in each of last 16dc, turn.
ROW 6: With Mint, 1ch, 1dc in each of first 15dc, with White, 1dc in each of last 5dc, turn.
ROW 7: With White, 1ch, 1dc in each of first 6dc, with Mint, 1dc in each of last 14dc, turn.
ROW 8: With Mint, 1ch, 1dc in each of first 13dc, with White, 1dc in each of last 7dc, turn.
ROW 9: With White, 1ch, 1dc in each of first 8dc, with Mint, 1dc in each of last 12dc, turn.
ROW 10: With Mint, 1ch, 1dc in each of first 11dc, with White, 1dc in each of last 9dc, turn.
ROW 11: With White, 1ch, 1dc in each of first 10dc, with Mint, 1dc in each of last 10dc, turn.
ROW 12: With Mint, 1ch, 1dc in each of first 9dc, with White, 1dc in each of last 11dc, turn.
ROW 13: With White, 1ch, 1dc in each of

first 12dc, with Mint, 1dc in each of last 8dc, turn.
ROW 14: With Mint, 1ch, 1dc in each of first 7dc, with White, 1dc in each of last 13dc, turn.
ROW 15: With White, 1ch, 1dc in each of first 14dc, with Mint, 1dc in each of last 6dc, turn.
ROW 16: With Mint, 1ch, 1dc in each of first 5dc, with White, 1dc in each of last 15dc, turn.
ROW 17: With White, 1ch, 1dc in each of first 16dc, with Mint, 1dc in each of last 4dc, turn.
ROW 18: With Mint, 1ch, 1dc in each of first 3dc, with White, 1dc in each of last 17dc, turn.
ROW 19: With White, 1ch, 1dc in each of first 18dc, with Mint, 1dc in each of last 2dc, turn.
ROW 20: With Mint, 1ch, 1dc in first dc, with White 1dc in each of last 19dc, turn.
ROW 21: With White, 1ch, 1dc in each of 20dc. Fasten off.
EDGING: With right side facing and using 3.5mm hook, join Lobster to first ch on base chain of motif and work 1dc in each of 20ch, 1ch for corner, 20dc along

row-end edge, 1ch for corner, 1dc in each of 20dc along fastened off edge, 1ch for corner, 20dc along other row-end edge, 1ch for corner, slst in first dc.
NEXT ROUND: [1dc in each dc to corner

chsp, work 1dc, 1ch and 1dc all in corner chsp] 4 times, slst in first dc. Fasten off.

TO MAKE UP

Arrange motifs in 6 rows of 7 motifs each. Working horizontally, place motifs with wrong sides together, using 3.5mm hook and Lobster, joining motifs by working slst into back loops of each corresponding pair of stitches. Join motifs vertically in same way.

BORDER

With right side facing and using 3.50 hook, join Lobster with slst to any corner chsp, 3ch (counts as 1tr), * 1tr in each of next 21dc, [tr2tog over next dc and chsp, tr2tog over next chsp and dc, 1dc in each of next 20dc] to last motif before corner, tr2tog over next dc and chsp, tr2tog over next chsp and dc, 1dc in each of next 21dc, work 1tr, 1ch, 1tr, 1ch and 1tr all in corner chsp, repeat from * 3 times more, ending with work 1tr, 1ch, 1tr and 1ch all in same chsp as slst, slst in top of 3ch ....(592 sts)

NEXT 3 ROUNDS: 3ch, [1tr in each tr to first chsp at corner, 1tr in chsp, work 1tr, 1ch, 1tr, 1ch and 1tr all in next tr, 1tr in next chsp] 4 times, slst in top of 3ch. Fasten off and neaten ends.

BOOTIES

MOTIF
(Make 2)

SIDES AND HEEL

With 3.5mm hook and White, ch 37.
ROW 1: 1dc in 2nd ch from hook, 1dc in each ch to end, turn. (36 sts)
ROWS 2-5: 1ch (does not count as a st throughout), 1dc in each dc to end, turn.
ROW 6: 3ch (counts as 1tr throughout), 1tr in each of next 6dc, 1htr in next dc, 1dc in each of next 20dc, 1htr in next dc, 1tr in each of last 7dc, turn.
ROW 7: 3ch, 1tr in each of next 7 sts, 1htr in next st, 1dc in each of next 18 sts, 1htr in next st, 1tr in each of last 8 sts, turn.
ROW 8: 1ch, 1htr in next st, [1ch, miss 1 st, 1htr in next st] to last st, slst in last st. Fasten off.
Instep: With 3.5mm hook and Mint, make 23ch.

ROW 1: 1dc in 2nd ch from hook, 1dc in each ch to end, turn. (22 sts)
ROWS 2-5: 1ch, 1dc in each of next 5 sts, dc2tog, [1dc in next st] to last 7dc, dc2tog, 1dc in each of last 5 sts, turn..(14 sts)
ROW 6: 1ch, 1dc in each of next 5 sts, [dc2tog twice, 1dc in each of last 5dc, turn ....(12 sts)
ROW 7: 1ch, 1dc in each of next 5 sts, dc2tog, 1dc in each of last 5 sts, turn..(11 sts)
ROW 8: 1ch, 1dc in each of next 3 sts, dc2tog, 1dc in next st, dc2tog, 1dc in each of last 3 sts, turn ....(9 sts)
ROW 9: 1ch, [miss 1 st, insert hook in next st, yrh and pull through] 4 times, yrh and pull through all 5 loops on hook, slst in last st.
Fasten off.
Sole: With 3.5mm hook and White, ch 13.
RND 1: 2dc in 2nd ch from hook, 1dc in each of next 10ch, 3dc in last ch, now work along other side of chain thus: 1dc in each of next 11ch, slst in first dc (26 sts)
RND 2: 1ch, 1dc in same dc as slst, 2dc in next dc, 1dc in each of next 10dc, 2dc in next dc, 1dc in next dc, 2dc in next dc, 1dc in each of next 10dc, 2dc in last dc, slst in first dc...................................(30 sts)
RND 3: 1ch, 1dc in same dc as slst, 2dc in next dc, 1dc in each of next 12dc, 2dc in next dc, 1dc in next dc, 2dc in next dc, 1dc in each of next 12dc, 2dc in last dc, slst in first dc...................................(34 sts)
RND 4: 1ch, 1dc in same dc as slst, 2dc in next dc, 1dc in each of next 14dc, 2dc in next dc, 1dc in next dc, 2dc in next dc, 1dc in each of next 14dc, 2dc in last dc, slst in first dc...................................(38 sts)

SHAPE FRONT

RND 5: 3ch, 2tr in next st, 1tr in next st, 2tr in next st, 1tr in each of next 4 sts, 1htr in next st, 1dc in each of next 5 sts, 1htr in each of next 2 sts, 2htr in next st, [1htr in next st, 2htr in next st] 3 times, 1htr in each of next 2 sts, 1dc in each of next 5 sts, 1htr in next st, 1tr in each of next 4 sts, 2tr in next st, 1tr in next st, 2tr in last st, slst in top of 3ch ....
....(46 sts)
RND 6: 3ch, 2htr in next st, [1htr in next st, 2htr in next st] twice, 1htr in each of next 4 sts, 1dc in each of next 7 sts, 1htr in each of next 3 sts, 2htr in next st, [1htr in next st, 2htr in next st] 3 times, 1htr in each of next 3 sts, 1dc in each of next 7

sts, 1htr in each of next 4 sts, [2htr in next st, 1htr in next st] twice, 2htr in last st, slst in top of 3ch ....56 sts)
Fasten off.

TO MAKE UP

1 With right side facing, using 3.5mm hook and Lobster, join row-ends at each side of instep to row-ends of sides and heel with slst, leaving last row on top free.

2 With right side facing, using 3.5mm hook and Lobster join sole in place by working slst into back loops of each corresponding pair of stitches.

3 With Lobster, make two 30cm-long twisted cords. Thread each along top edge, bringing ends at front.

TOY

BODY

With 3.5mm hook and White, ch 42, making sure that the chain is not twisted, slst in first ch to form ring.
RND 1: 1dc in each ch to end, slst in first dc.
RND 2: 1ch (does not count as a st throughout entire instructions), [2dc in next dc, 1dc in each of next 6dc] 6 times, slst in first dc.................................. (48 sts)
RND 3: 1ch, [2dc in next dc, 1dc in each of next 7dc] 6 times, slst in first dc .... (54 sts)
RND 4: 1ch, [2dc in next dc, 1dc in each of next 8dc] 6 times, slst in first dc .... (60 sts)
RND 5: 1ch, [2dc in next dc, 1dc in each of next 9dc] 6 times, slst in first dc .... (66 sts)
RND 6: 1ch, [2dc in next dc, 1dc in each of next 10dc] 6 times, slst in first dc(72 sts)
RND 7: 1ch, [2dc in next dc, 1dc in each of next 11dc] 6 times, slst in first dc(78 sts)
RNDS 8-10: 1ch, 1dc in each dc to end, slst in first dc.
RND 11: 1ch, [dc2tog, 1dc in each of next 11 sts] 6 times, slst in first st......................
.... (72 sts)
RND 12: 1ch, [dc2tog, 1dc in each of next 10 sts] 6 times, slst in first st...............(66 sts)
RND 13: 1ch, [dc2tog, 1dc in each of next 9 sts] 6 times, slst in first st............. (60 sts)
RND 14: 1ch, [dc2tog, 1dc in each of next

8 sts] 6 times, slst in first st............ (54 sts)
RND 15: 1ch, [dc2tog, 1dc in each of next 7 sts] 6 times, slst in first st.............. (48 sts)
RND 16: 1ch, [dc2tog, 1dc in each of next 6 sts] 6 times, slst in first st.............. (42 sts)
Fasten off.
Join chain edge and fastened-off edge together, stuffing body as you work.

SNOUT
With 3.5mm hook and Mint, ch 5.
RND 1: 2dc in 2nd ch from hook, 1dc in each of next 2ch, 3dc in last ch, now work along other side of chain thus: 1dc in each of next 3ch, slst in first dc. ....
.... (10 sts)
RND 2: 1ch, 1dc in same dc as slst, 2dc in next dc, 1dc in each of next 2dc, 2dc in next dc, 1dc in next dc, 2dc in next dc, 1dc in each of next 2dc, 2dc in last dc, slst in first dc................................. (14 sts)
RND 3: 1ch, 1dc in same dc as slst, 2dc in next dc, 1dc in each of next 4dc, 2dc in

next dc, 1dc in next dc, 2dc in next dc, 1dc in each of next 4dc, 2dc in last dc, slst in first dc................................. (18 sts)
RNDS 4-5: 1ch, 1dc in each dc to end, slst in first dc. Fasten off.
Stuff and sew snout to centre at top of body. With Lobster, embroider nose on snout. Work French knot in Black on body at each side of snout for eyes.

EARS
(Make 2)
RND 1: With 3.5mm hook and Lobster, make a slip ring as follows: wind yarn round index finger of left hand to form a ring, insert hook into ring, yarn over hook and pull through, 1ch, 6dc in ring, slst in 1ch, pull end of yarn tightly to close ring.. (6 sts)
Mark end of round and move marker up at end of every round.
RND 2: [2dc in next dc] 6 times..... (12 sts)
RND 3: [2dc in next dc, 1dc in next dc] 6 times... (18 sts) **

RND 4: [2dc in next dc, 1dc in each of next 2dc] 6 times........................... (24 sts)
Fold ear in half.
NEXT ROW: 1ch, work through corresponding pair of stitches thus: [2dc in next st, 1dc in each of next 3 sts] 3 times. Fasten off.
Sew ears to top of body as shown in the photo.

ARMS
(Make 2)
With White, work as ears to **.
RNDS 4-5: [1dc in next dc] to end.
RNDS 6-7: [Dc2tog, 1dc in next st] to end 8 sts)
Fasten off.
Stuff arms lightly and sew fastened-off edge to each side of body as shown in photo.

Pattern by:

Olive's Toy Box

Olive's Toy Box specialises in crochet designs for babies and children. All the patterns are easy to follow, quick to make and suitable for beginners. With Olive's Toy Box patterns, you can create special little friends to be loved and cherished for years to come.

www.facebook.com/ Olivestoybox

You Will Need...

Yarn:
- You will need to use DK weight yarn in your chosen colours. Here we have used Paintbox Yarn Cotton DK in:
- Colour 1: 452 Lipstick Pink
- Colour 2: 404 Misty Grey
- Colour 3: 402 Pure Black
- A selection of colours for the spikes: 429, 434, 423, 451, 433, 414, 443
- James C Brett Flutterby Chunky, 100g: Colour 4: B36 Parchment

Tools:
- 3mm hook (US C)
- 4mm (US G/6)
- Yarn needle
- Scissors
- Stitch markers

Other:
- Fibrefill stuffing

Optional:
- Squeakers, bells, rattles, buttons, beads etc to put inside the toy

HEDGEHOG SENSORY TOY

HELP DEVELOP YOUR BABY'S SENSES WITH THIS NOT-SO-PRICKLY CRITTER

Pattern

Finished product size: approx. 30cm long

* **GAUGE:** 2.5cm/1in approx: 5dc/5 rows (Flutterby), 7dc/7rows (Paintbox)
* **NOTE:** Rounds are worked in a continous spiral; do not join. Mark the end of each round with a stitch marker.

HEAD

Using 3mm hook and col 1, magic a magic ring.
RND 1: 6 dc in magic ring. (6 sts)
RND 2: 2 dc in each st .... (12 sts)
RND 3: (1 dc in next st, 2 dc in next st) 6 times.................................... (18 sts)
RND 4: 1 dc in next 2 sts, 2 dc in next st) 6 times................................... (24 sts)
RNDS 5-7: 1 dc in each st .... (24 sts)
RND 8: (1 dc in next 6 sts, dc2tog) 3 times.. (21 sts)
Change to col 2.
RND 9: 1 dc in each st .... (21 sts)
RND 10: (1 dc in next 6 sts, 2 dc in next st) 6 times.................................... (24 sts)

Put a button or bead inside.
Close up the nose.

Flatten your work, so the first stitch of the next round is on the right side. Use approx 30cm of col 1 yarn to stitch up the nose, under RND 9.

You can also put something inside, like a plastic button or a little bead, to make it more interesting for babies.

RND 11: 1 dc in next 12 sts, then (1 dc in next st, 2 dc in next st) 6 times.........(30 sts)
RND 12-13: 1 dc in each st ....(30 sts)
RND 14: 1 dc in next 12 sts, then (1 dc in next 2 sts, 2 dc in next st) 6 times .... (36 sts)
RND 15: 1 dc in each st ....(36 sts)
RND 16: 1 dc in next 12 sts, then (1 dc in next 3 sts, 2 dc in next st) 6 times... (42 scs)
RND 17: 1 dc in next 12 sts, then (1 dc in next 4 sts, 2 dc in next st) 6 times ...(48 sts)
RND 18: 1 dc in next 12 sts, then (1 dc in next 5 sts, 2 dc in next st) 6 times....(54 sts)
RNDS 19-23: 1 dc in each st.........(54 sts)
Don't fasten off, move on to the instructions for the Body.

BODY

Use 3mm hook and col 4.
RND 1: 1 dc in each st ....(54 sts)
Change hook to 4mm.
RND 2: (1 dc in next 7 sts, dc2tog) 6 times..(48 sts)
RND 3: dc2tog 6 times, 1 dc in next 36 sts ....(42 sts)
RNDS 4-20: 1 dc in each st ....(42 sts)
Start stuffing.
RND 21: (1 dc in next 5 sts, dc2tog) 6 times..(36 sts)

Crochet TOYBOX

Creating the nose

RND 22: (1 dc in next 4 sts, dc2tog)
6 times...(30 sts)
RND 23: (1 dc in next 3 sts, dc2tog)
6 times...(24 sts)
RND 24: (1 dc in next 2 sts, dc2tog)
6 times.. (18 sts)
RND 25: (1 dc in next st, dc2tog)
6 times .... (12 sts)
RND 26: dc2tog 6 times ....(6 sts)
Make sure you have enough stuffing
inside and fasten off

LEGS
(Make 2)
Using 3mm hook and col 2, make magic
ring.
RND 1: 6 dc in magic ring.............(6sts)
RND 2: 2 dc in each st ....(12sts)
RND 3: (1 dc in next st, 2 dc in next st) 6
times..(18sts)
RNDS 4-12: 1 dc in each st ....(18sts)
Do not stuff.
Fasten off, leaving 30cm tail for sewing.

SPIKES
(Make 7)
Make 1 spike in each colour.
Using 3mm hook, make magic ring.
RND 1: 6 dc in magic ring.............(6 sts)
RND 2: (1 dc in each st, 2 dc in each st)
3 times...(9 sts)
RND 3: (1 dc in next 2 sts, 2 dc in next
st) 3 times...................................(12 sts)
RND 4: (1 dc in next 3 sts, 2 dc in next
st) 3 times...................................(15 sts)
RND 5: (1 dc in next 4 sts, 2 dc in next
st) 3 times...................................(18 sts)
RND 6: (1 dc in next 5 sts, 2 dc in next
st) 3 times...................................(21 sts)
RND 7: (1 dc in next 6 sts, 2 dc in next
st) 3 times...................................(24 sts)
RND 8: (1 dc in next 7 sts, 2 dc in next

st) 3 times....................................(27 sts)
RND 9: (1 dc in next 8 sts, 2 dc in next
st) 3 times...................................(30 sts)
RND 10: (1 dc in next 9 sts, 2 dc in next
st) 3 times...................................(33 sts)
RND 11: 1 dc in each st...............(33 sts)
Do not stuff.
Fasten off, leaving 30cm tail for sewing.

ASSEMBLY

1 Attach the spikes, approx. 2 RNDs away from the head. Three spikes along the middle of the body and two spikes on each side (approx 7 sts away from the middle row of spikes). You can put little squeakers, beads or buttons inside them, before attaching the spikes to the body.

2 Attach the legs, approx. 1 RND away from the head, 6 st down from the side rows of spikes.

3 Embroider the eyes using col 3, 6 sts away from the centre of the face, between RNDs 17 and 21 of the head.

Legs

Spikes

Nose

KOALA TEETHER & RATTLE

CREATE THIS CUTE TEETHER AND RATTLE
THE PERFECT GIFT FOR ANY BABY

Pattern by:

CrochetByKim

CrochetByKim is a Swedish amigurumi designer who has been making patterns since 2017. She crochets every day and sees it as a therapy for her full-time job as a 911 dispatcher.

@crochetbykim

You Will Need...

Yarn:
- 4 ply or fingering super fine cotton yarn in your chosen colours. Here we have used 1 ball each of Hobbii Rainbow Cotton in:
  - Light Grey
  - Dark Grey
  - White
  - Mint
  - Black

Tools:
- 2.5mm hook (US C/2)
- Yarn needle
- Scissors

Other:
- Toy stuffing
- 2 plastic rattle balls
- 5.5mm (2.1in) wooden ring

Pattern

Finished product size: Teether: 12cm (4.7in) long; 12cm (4.7in) wide; 7cm (2.7in) deep
Rattle: 15cm (5.9in) long; 12cm (4.7in) wide; 7cm (2.7in) deep

* **GAUGE:** Is not critical for this pattern. Using 2.5mm hook with 4 ply or fingering weight yarn will create a tight stitch so that the stuffing does not show through.
* **NOTES:** Work in the round without turning or joining. Using a stitch marker to mark the beginning of each round will make it easier to keep track of which round you're working on.

TEETHER

HEAD

Using col 1, make a magic ring.
RND 1: Ch 1, work 6 dc into the ring. ...
....(6 sts)
RND 2: 2 dc in each st .... (12 sts)
RND 3: (1 dc in next st, 2 dc in next st) 6 times..(18 sts)
RND 4: (1 dc in next 2 sts, 2 dc in next st) 6 times...................................(24 sts)
RND 5: (1 dc in next 3 sts, 2 dc in next st) 6 times...................................(30 sts)
RND 6: (1 dc in next 4 sts, 2 dc in next st) 6 times...................................(36 sts)
RND 7: (1 dc in next 5 sts, 2 dc in next st) 6 times...................................(42 sts)
RND 8: (1 dc in next 6 sts, 2 dc in next st) 6 times...................................(48 sts)
RNDS 9-15: 1 dc in each st...........(48 sts)
RND 16: (1 dc in next 6 sts, dc2tog) 6 times..(42 sts)
RND 17: (1 dc in next 5 sts, dc2tog) 6 times..(36 sts)
RND 18: (1 dc in next 4 sts, dc2tog) 6 times..(30 sts)
RND 19: (1 dc in next 3 sts, dc2tog) 6 times..(24 sts)
RND 20: (1 dc in next 2 sts, dc2tog) 6 times..(18 sts)
RND 21: (1 dc in next st, dc2tog) 6 times..(12 sts)
RND 22: Dc2tog 6 times. (6 sts)
Fasten off and weave in ends.

NOSE

Using col 2, ch 5.
RND 1 (RS): 1 dc in 2nd ch from hook, 1 dc in next 2 sts, 4 dc in next st, turn and work along opposite side of the foundation chain: 1 dc in next 2 sts, 3 dc in next st.....................................(12 sts)
RND 2: 2 dc in next st, 1 dc in next 3 sts, 2 dc in next st, 1 dc in next st, 2 dc in next st, 1 dc in next 3 sts, 2 dc in next st, 1 dc in next st........................(16 sts)
RND 3: 2 dc in next st, 1 dc in next 5 sts, 2 dc in next st, 1 dc in next st, 2 dc in next st, 1 dc in next 5 sts, 2 dc in next st, 1 dc in next st........................(20 sts)
RNDS 4-6: 1 dc in each st...........(20 sts)

Ss in next st and fasten off, leaving a tail for sewing.

Pin and sew the nose onto the head between rnds 10 and 17.

Embroider the eyes on the head over 2 sts between rnds 10 and 11.

EARS

(Make 2)
Using col 1, make a magic ring.
RND 1 (RS): Ch1, work 6 dc into the ring (6 sts)
RND 2: 2 dc in each st .... (12 sts)
RND 3: (1 dc in next st, 2 dc in next st) 6

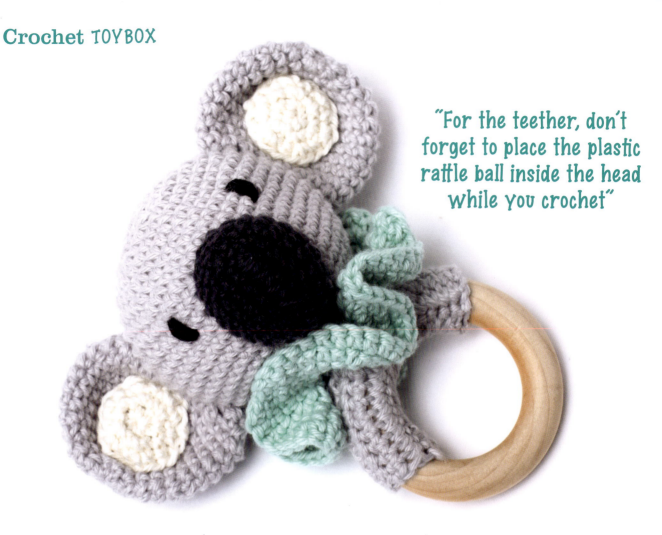

"For the teether, don't forget to place the plastic rattle ball inside the head while you crochet"

times...(18 sts)
RND 4: (1 dc in next 2 sts, 2 dc in next st) 6 times...................................(24 sts)
RND 5: (1 dc in next 3 sts, 2 dc in next st) 6 times...................................(30 sts)
RNDS 6-10: 1 dc in each st. (30 sts)
Rnd 11: (1 dc in next 3 sts, dc2tog) 6 times..(24 sts)
Rnd 12: (1 dc in next 2 sts, dc2tog) 6 times..(18 sts)
Ss in next st and fasten off, leaving a tail for sewing.

INNER EAR
(Make 2)
Using col 3, make a magic ring.
RND 1 (RS): Ch 1, work 6 dc into the ring ....(6 sts)
RND 2: 2 dc in each st ....(12 sts)
RND 3: (1 dc in next st, 2 dc in next st) 6 times...(18 sts)
Ss in next st and fasten off, leaving a tail for sewing.

Sew the inner ears onto the ears before pinning and attaching to koala head

between rnds 7 and 15.

COLLAR
Using col 4, make a magic ring.
RND 1 (RS): Ch 1, work 6 dc into the ring ....(6 sts)
RND 2: 2 dc in each st ....(12 sts)
RND 3: (1 dc in next st, 2 dc in next st) 6 times...(18 sts)
RND 4: (1 dc in next 2 sts, 2 dc in next st) 6 times...................................(24 sts)
RND 5: 2 dc in each st ....(48 sts)
RND 6: (1 dc in next st, 2 dc in next st) 24 times....................................(72 sts)
RND 7: (1 dc in next st, 2 dc in next st) 36 times....................................(108 sts)
RND 8: 1 dc in each st ....(108 sts)

Ss in next st and fasten off, leaving a tail for sewing.

Pin and sew rnds 3 and 4 of the collar on the underside of the koala's head.

RIBBON
Using col 1, ch 20, turn.

ROW 1 (RS): 1 dc in 2nd ch from hook, 1 dc in each st to end, turn.
....(19 sts)
ROWS 2-9: Ch 1 (does not count as a st), 1 dc in each st to end, turn ....(19 sts)

Fasten off, leaving a tail for sewing.

Sew the ribbon around the wooden ring, and turn the seam to the inside of the ring. Sew the head onto the ribbon.

RATTLE

HEAD/HANDLE

Using col 1, make a magic ring and work as given for teether Head up to the end of row 20 ....(18 sts)

RND 21: In front loops only, 1 dc in each st..(18 sts)

Stuff the head and put bell inside. Continue stuffing as you go along.

RNDS 22-34: 1 dc in each st.......(18 sts)

RND 35: (1 dc in next 2 sts, 2 dc in next st) 6 times..........................(24 sts)

RND 36: (1 dc in next 3 sts, 2 dc in next st) 6 times...................................(30 sts)

RNDS 37-41: 1 dc in each st ....(30 sts)

RND 42: (1 dc in next 3 sts, dc2tog) 6 times..(24 sts)

RND 43: (1 dc in next 2 sts, dc2tog) 6 times..(18 sts)

RND 44: (1 dc in next st, dc2tog) 6 times..(12 sts)

RND 45: dc2tog 6 times...............(6 sts)

Fasten off, leaving a tail for sewing.

NOSE

Using col 2, work as given for teether nose.

Pin and sew the nose onto the head between rnds 10 and 17.

Embroider the eyes on the head over 2 sts between rnds 10 and 11.

EARS

(Make 2)

Using col 1, work as given for teether ears.

INNER EAR

(Make 2)

Using col 3, work as given for teether inner ears.

Sew inner ears to ears before pinning and attaching to rattle between rnds 7 and 15.

PATCH

Using col 3, ch 7.

RND 1 (RS): 1 dc in 2nd ch from hook, 1 dc in next 4 sts, 4 dc in next st. Turn and work along opposite side of the foundation chain: 1 dc in next 4 sts, 3 dc in next st............ (16 sts)

RND 2: 2 dc in next st, 1 dc in next 5 sts, 2 dc in next st, 1 dc in next st, 2 dc in next st, 1 dc in next 5 sts, 2 dc in next st, 1 dc in next st..(20 sts)

Ss in next st and fasten off, leaving a tail for sewing.

Pin and sew patch to rattles between rnds 22 and 31 on handle.

LAMB LOVEY

CREATE THIS CUTE AND CUDDLY LAMB LOVEY
THE PERFECT GIFT FOR ANY BABY

Pattern by:

Ariana Wimsett

Ariana is the crochet designer behind Crafting Happiness. She specialises in nursery decor, blankets and amigurumi toys, and her patterns are fun and easy to make, designed with the beginner crocheter in mind.

craftinghappiness.com

www.facebook.com/
CraftingHappinessCrochet

www.ravelry.com/designers/
crafting-happiness

You Will Need...

Yarn:
- You will need to use DK yarn in your chosen colour. Here we have used Deramores Studio DK in:
- Colour 1: White (3 balls)
- Colour 2: Grey (1 ball)

Tools:
- 4.5mm hook (US 7)
- Yarn needle
- Fibrefill stuffing
- A pair of 10mm black safety eyes

Pattern

Finished product size: 55cm (21¾in) diameter
Tension: 16 sts x 16 rows to measure 10x10cm (4x4in), over pattern using 4.5mm hook

- **BOBBLE STITCH (BO):** *Yoh, insert hook into stitch or space indicated, yoh and pull a loop through so you now have 3 loops on your hook. Yoh and pull through 2 loops. Repeat this step from *, 4 more times in the same stitch or space, until you have 6 loops on your hook. Yoh and pull through all 6 loops.
- **MODIFIED BOBBLE STITCH (MBO):** This is almost identical to the regular bobble stitch (bo), but it uses 4 unfinished tr stitches clustered together in the same stitch instead of the regular 5 (therefore having 5 loops on your hook before the final yoh).
- **THREE TREBLE CROCHET CLUSTER (TR3CL):** 3 tr stitches in the same stitch/space.
- **CORNER 1:** (1 tr, ch 2, 1 tr) in the same stitch (for round 3) or chain space (for rest of rounds).
- **CORNER 2:** (2 dc, ch 2, 2 dc) in the same chain space.
- **DEC:** work a dc2tog as follows: insert hook in first st, yoh and pull a loop through, insert hook in next st, yoh and pull a loop through, yoh and pull through all 3 loops.
- **NOTE:** In each round, the corner chains are included in the stitch count. You only join the round on rnd 2 and following alternate rounds.after 2nd bracket.

PATTERN
STAR-SHAPED LOVEY

Using col 1, make a magic ring.
RND 1 (RS): Work 10 dc into the ring..(10 sts)
RND 2: ([1 dc and 1 tr3cl] in next st) 10 times, ss into 1st st.......................(20 sts)
RND 3: (1 dc in next st, Corner 1 in next st, 1 dc in next st, sk next st) 5 times, ss into 1st st......................................(30 sts)
RND 4: (1 dc in next st, Corner 2 in next st, 1 dc in next st, dec) 5 times ....
....(45 sts)
RND 5: (1 dc in next st, mbo in next st, 1 dc in next st, Corner 1 in next st, 1 dc in next st, mbo in next st, 1 dc in next st, sk next st) 5 times, ss into 1st st ... (50 sts)
RND 6: (1 dc in next 3 sts, Corner 2 in next st, 1 dc in next 3 sts, dec) 5 times .. (65 sts)
RND 7: ([1 dc in next st, mbo in next st] twice, 1 dc in next st, Corner 1 in next

st, 1 dc in next st, [mbo in next st, 1 dc in next st] twice, sk 1 st) 5 times, ss in 1st st..(70 sts)
RND 8: (1 dc in next 5 sts, Corner 2 in next st, 1 dc in next 5 sts, dec) 5 times.. (85 sts)
RND 9: ([1 dc in next st, mbo in next st] 3 times, 1 dc in next st, Corner 1 in next st, 1 dc in next st, [mbo in next st, 1 dc in next st] 3 times, sk 1 st) 5 times, ss into 1st st......................................(90 sts)
RND 10: (1 dc into next 7 sts, Corner 2 in next st, 1 dc in next 7 sts, dec) 5 times...(105 sts)
RND 11: ([1 dc in next st, mbo in next st] 4 times, 1 dc in next st, Corner 1 in next st, 1 dc in next st, [mbo in next st, 1 dc in next st] 4 times, sk 1 st) 5 times, ss into 1st st.................................... (110 sts)
RND 12: (1 dc in next 9 sts, Corner 2 in next st, 1 dc in next 9 sts, dec) 5 times .. (125 sts)
RND 13: ([1 dc in next st, mbo in next st]

1 dc in next st] 10 times, sk 1 st) 5 times, ss into 1st st...............................(230 sts)

RND 24: (1 dc in next 21 sts, Corner 2 in next st, 1 dc in next 21 sts, dec) 5 times (245 sts)

RND 25: ([1 dc in next st, mbo in next st] 11 times, 1 dc in next st, Corner 1 in next st, 1 dc in next st, [mbo in next st, 1 dc in next st] 11 times, sk 1 st) 5 times, ss into 1st st...............................(250 sts)

RND 26: (1 dc in next 23 sts, Corner 2 in next st, 1 dc in next 23 sts, dec) 5 times (265 sts)

RND 27: ([1 dc in next st, mbo in next st] 12 times, 1 dc in next st, Corner 1 in next st, 1 dc in next st, [mbo in next st, 1 dc in next st] 12 times, sk 1 st) 5 times, ss into 1st st...............................(270 sts)

RND 28: (1 dc in next 25 sts, Corner 2 in next st, 1 dc in next 25 sts, dec) 5 times (285 sts)

RND 29: ([1 dc in next st, mbo in next st] 13 times, 1 dc in next st, Corner 1 in next st, 1 dc in next st, [mbo in next st, 1 dc in next st] 13 times, sk 1 st) 5 times, ss into 1st st...............................(290 sts)
Change to col 2.

RND 30: (1 dc in next 27 sts, Corner 2 in next st, 1 dc in next 27 sts, dec) 5 times (305 sts)

RND 31: (1 dc in next 29 sts, Corner 2 in next st, 1 dc in next 29 sts, sk 1 st) 5 times..(320 sts)
Finish off and weave in ends.

HEAD
Using col 2, make a magic ring.
RND 1 (RS): Work 6 dc into the ring ....(6 sts)
RND 2: 2 dc in each st ....(12 sts)
RND 3: (2 dc in next st, 1 dc in next st) 6 time ....(18 sts)
RND 4: (2 dc in next st, 1 dc in next 2 sts) 6 times ....(24 sts)
RNDS 5-6: 1 dc in each st............(24 sts)
RND 7: (2 dc in next st, 1 dc in next 3 sts) 6 times ....(30 sts)
RNDS 8-9: 1 dc in each st............(30 sts)
RND 10: (2 dc in next st, 1 dc in next 4 sts) 6 times ....(36 sts)
RNDS 11-12: 1 dc in each st.........(36 sts)
Change to col 1.
RND 13: 1 dc in each st ....(36 sts)
RND 14: (1 dc in next st, 1 bo in next st) to end...(36 sts)
RND 15: (2 dc in next st, 1 dc in next 3 sts) 9 times ....(45 sts)
RND 16: (1 dc in next st, 1 bo in next st)

5 times, 1 dc in next st, Corner 1 in next st, 1 dc in next st, [mbo in next st, 1 dc in next st] 5 times, sk 1 st) 5 times, ss into 1st st ....(130 sts)

RND 14: (1 dc in next 11 sts, Corner 2 in next st, 1 dc in next 11 sts, dec) 5 times (145 sts)

RND 15: ([1 dc in next st, mbo in next st] 6 times, 1 dc in next st, Corner 1 in next st, 1 dc in next st, [mbo in next st, 1 dc in next st] 6 times, sk 1 st) 5 times, ss into 1st st...................................(150 sts)

RND 16: (1 dc in next 13 sts, Corner 2 in next st, 1 dc in next 13 sts, dec) 5 times (165 sts)

RND 17: ([1 dc in next st, mbo in next st] 7 times, 1 dc in next st, Corner 1 in next st, 1 dc in next st, [mbo in next st, 1 dc in next st] 7 times, sk 1 st) 5 times, ss into 1st st...................................(170 sts)

RND 18: (1 dc in next 15 sts, Corner 2 in next st, 1 dc in next 15 sts, dec) 5 times (185 sts)

RND 19: ([1 dc in next st, mbo in next st] 8 times, 1 dc in next st, Corner 1 in next st, 1 dc in next st, [mbo in next st, 1 dc in next st] 8 times, sk 1 st) 5 times, ss into 1st st....................................(190 sts)

RND 20: (1 dc in next 17 sts, Corner 2 in next st, 1 dc in next 17 sts, dec) 5 times (205 sts)

RND 21: ([1 dc in next st, mbo in next st] 9 times, 1 dc in next st, Corner 1 in next st, 1 dc in next st, [mbo in next st, 1 dc in next st] 9 times, sk 1 st) 5 times, ss into next st ....(210 sts)

RND 22: (1 dc in next 19 sts, Corner 2 in next st, 1 dc in next 19 sts, dec) 5 times (225 sts)

RND 23: ([1 dc in next st, mbo in next st] 10 times, 1 dc in next st, Corner 1 in next st, 1 dc in next st, [mbo in next st,

to last st, 1 dc in last st ....(45 sts)
RND 17: 1 dc in each st..............(45 sts)
RND 18: 1 bo in next st, (1 dc in next st, 1 bo in next st) to end.................(45 sts)
RND 19: 1 dc in each st ....(45 sts)
RND 20: 1 bo in next st, (1 dc in next st, 1 bo in next st) to end.................(45 sts)
RND 21: (Dec, 1 dc in next 3 sts) 9 times (36 sts)
Place the eyes 10 stitches apart, between rnds 10 and 11. Start filling the head with fibrefill and continue stuffing as you work.
RND 22: (1 dc in next st, 1 bo in next st) to end............................(36 sts)
RND 23: (Dec, 1 dc in next 2 sts) 9 times (27 sts)
RND 24: 1 bo in next st, (1 dc in next st, 1 bo in next st) to end.................(27 sts)
RND 25: (Dec, 1 dc in next st) 9 times...............................(18 sts)
RND 26: (1 dc in next st, 1 bo in next st) to end............................(18 sts)
RND 27: (Dec, 1 dc in next st) 6 times. . (12 sts)
RND 28: (1 dc in next st, 1 bo in next st) 6 times..........................(12 sts)
Fasten off and finish filling up the head. Cut the yarn leaving a long tail, and use it to close up the hole in the head.

EARS
(Make 2)
Using col 2, make a magic ring.
RND 1: Work 6 dc into the ring ....(6 sts)
RND 2: 2 dc in each st ....(12 sts)
RND 3: (2 dc in next st, 1 dc in next st) 6 times...(18 sts)
RNDS 4-8: 1 dc in each st............(18 sts)
RND 9: (Dec, 1 dc in next st) 6 times. ....(12 sts)
RNDS 10-12: 1 dc in each st ....(12 sts)
Flatten ear and ss through both layers. Finish off, leaving a long tail for sewing.

LEGS
(Make 2)
Using col 2, make a magic ring.
RND 1: Work 6 dc into the ring .....(6 sts)
RND 2: 2 dc in each st ....(12 sts)
RND 3: (2 dc in next st, 1 dc in next st) 6 times...(18 sts)
RND 4: (2 dc in next st, 1 dc in next 5 sts) 3 times ....(21 sts)
RNDS 5-9: 1 dc in each st............(21 sts)
Change to col 1.
RND 10: 1 dc in each st ....(21 sts)
RND 11: 1 dc in next 19 sts, dec.
....(20 sts)
RND 12: 1 dc in each st ....(20 sts)
RND 13: 1 dc in next 9 sts, dec, 1 dc in next 9 sts......................................(19 sts)

RND 14: 1 dc in each st ....(19 sts)
RND 15: 1 dc in next 17 sts, dec......(18 sts)
RND 16: 1 dc in each st ....(18 sts)
Start stuffing the leg with fibrefill. Continue stuffing as you work.
RND 17: 1 dc in next 8 sts, dec, 1 dc in next 8 sts.....................................(17 sts)
RND 18: 1 dc in each st ....(17 sts)
RND 19: 1 dc in next 15 sts, dec.
....(16 sts)
RND 20: 1 dc in each st ....(16 sts)
RND 21: 1 dc in next 7 sts, dec, 1 dc in next 7 sts ....(15 sts)
RND 22: 1 dc in each st ....(15 sts)
RND 23: 1 dc in next 13 sts, dec.....(14 sts)
RND 25: 1 dc in each st ....(14 sts)
Finish filling leg, flatten edge and ss through both layers. Finish off, leaving a long tail for sewing.

ASSEMBLY
1 Fold each ear in half and sew a couple of stitches through the base, then sew them onto the head.

2 Sew the head in the centre of the star.

3 The two arms are attached to the star on either side of the head.

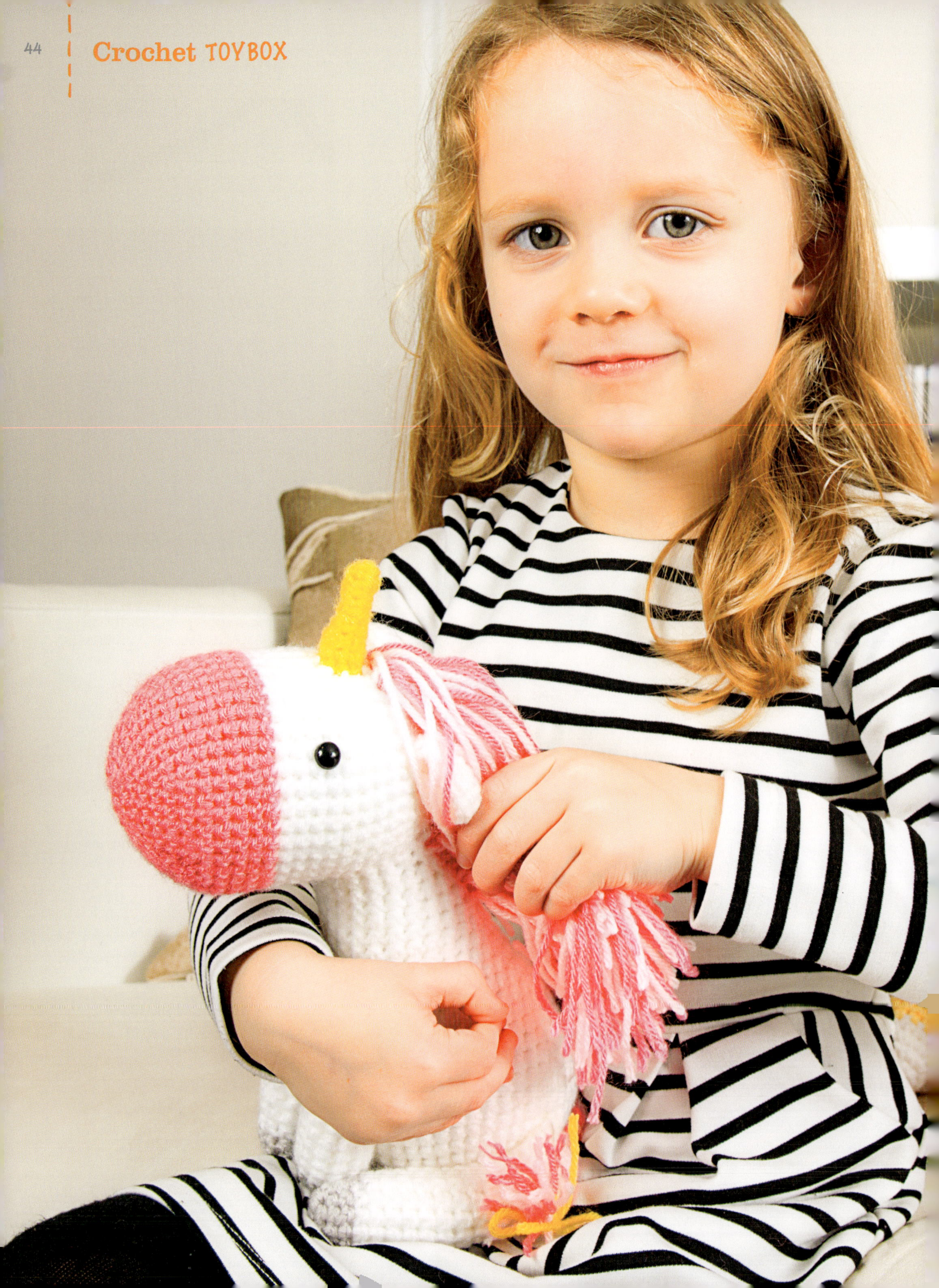

ANIMALS

PIG PLUSHIE

THIS ADORABLE PIG IS THE PERFECT COMPANION FOR ANYONE WHO LOVES CUDDLY TOYS

Pattern

Finished product size: Approximately 24cm/9½in tall, excluding ears.

★ This pattern is worked in a continuous spiral unless otherwise specified. Mark the end of each round with a stitch marker.

★ **NOTE:** Yarn amounts are based on average requirements and are therefore approximate. Instructions in square brackets are worked as stated after 2nd bracket.

BODY

With 4mm hook, ch 2.
RND 1: 6dc in 2nd ch from hook... (6 sts)
RND 2: (2 dc in next st) 6 times...(12 sts)
RND 3: (2 dc in next st, 1 dc in next st) 6 times..................................(18 sts)
RND 4: (2 dc in next st, 1 dc in next 2 sts) 6 times .... (24 sts)
RND 5: (2 dc in next st, 1 dc in next 3 sts) 6 times .... (30 sts)
RND 6: (2 dc in next st, 1 dc in next 4 sts) 6 times .... (36 sts)
RND 7: (2 dc in next st, 1 dc in next 5 sts) 6 times .... (42 sts)
RND 8: (2 dc in next st, 1 dc in next 6 sts) 6 times .... (48 sts)
RND 9: (2 dc in next st, 1 dc in next 7 sts) 6 times .... (54 sts)
RNDS 10-13: 1 dc in each st .... (54 sts)
RND 14: (dc2tog, 1 dc in next 7 sts) 6 times... (48 sts)
RNDS 15-17: 1 dc in each st .... (48 sts)
RND 18: (dc2tog, 1 dc in next 6 sts) 6 times... (42 sts)
RNDS 19-20: 1 dc in each st....... (42 sts)
RND 21: (dc2tog, 1 dc in next 5 sts) 6 times... (36 sts)
RNDS 22-23: 1 dc in each st....... (36 sts)
RND 24: (dc2tog, 1 dc in next 4 sts) 6 times... (30 sts)
RND 25: 1 dc in each st .... (30 sts)
RND 26: (dc2tog, 1 dc in next 3 sts) 6 times... (24 sts)

RND 27: 1 dc in each st .... (24 sts)
RND 28: (dc2tog, 1 dc in next 2 sts) 6 times...(18 sts)
Stuff body firmly, adding more stuffing as you working last 2 rounds.
RND 29: (dc2tog, 1 dc in next st] 6 times...(12 sts)
RND 30: dc2tog 6 times............... (6 sts)
Fasten off for top edge.
Gather fastened-off edge, pull up tightly and secure.

HEAD

With 4mm hook, ch 2.
RND 1: 6dc in 2nd ch from hook .....(6 sts)
RND 2: 2 dc in each st ....(12 sts)
RND 3: (2 dc in next st, 1 dc in next st) 6 times.................................(18 sts)
RND 4: 1 dc in back loop of each st. .... (18 sts)
RNDS 5-7: 1 dc in each st ....(18 sts)
RND 8: (2 dc in next st, 1 dc in next 2 sts) 6 times .... (24 sts.)
RND 9: 1 dc in each st .... (24 sts)
RND 10: (2 dc in next st, 1 dc in next 3 sts 6 times .... (30 sts)
RND 11: 1 dc in each st............... (30 sts)
RND 12: (2 dc in next st, 1 dc in next 4 sts) 6 times .... (36 sts)
RND 13: 1 dc in each st .... (36 sts)
RND 14: (2 dc in next st, 1 dc in next 5 sts) 6 times .... (42 sts)
RND 15: (2 dc in next st, 1 dc in next 6 sts) 6 times .... (48 sts)

RNDS 16-19: 1 dc in each st .... (48 sts)
RND 20: (dc2tog, 1 dc in next 6 sts) 6 times.. (42 sts)
RND 21: (dc2tog, 1 dc in next 5 sts) 6 times.. (36 sts)
RND 22: (dc2tog, 1 dc in next 4 sts) 6 times.. (30 sts)
RND 23: (dc2tog, 1 dc in next 3 sts) 6 times.. (24 sts)
RND 24: (dc2tog, 1 dc in next 2 sts) 6 times..(18 sts)
Stuff head firmly.
RND 25: (dc2tog, 1 dc in next st) 6 times..(12 sts)
RND 26: dc2tog 6 times.............. (6 sts)
Fasten off for back of head.
Gather fastened-off edge, pull up tightly and secure. Sew head to top of body.
With Green, embroider eyes.

LEGS

(Make 2)
With 4mm hook, ch 2.
RND 1: 6dc in 2nd ch from hook.... (6 sts)
RND 2: 2 dc in each st...................(12 sts)
RNDS 3-14: 1 dc in each st ....(12 sts)
Fasten off.
Stuff legs, flatten tops and sew to base of body.

ARMS

(Make 2)
With 4mm hook, ch 2.
RND 1: 6dc in 2nd ch from hook.... (6 sts)
RND 2: 2dc in each st ....(12 sts)
RNDS 3-11: 1 dc in each st ....(12 sts)
Fasten off.
Stuff arms, flatten tops and sew to sides of body. Stitch hands together at centre front

TAIL

With 4mm hook, ch 11.
ROW 1: 1dc in 2nd ch from hook, 1dc in each of next 9ch.

You Will Need...

Materials:
- 1 x 50g (116m) ball of Sublime Baby Cashmere
- Merino Silk DK (75% merino wool, 20% silk, 5% cashmere) in Piglet (01)*
- Small amount in Green for embroidery

Tools:
- 4mm hook (US G-6)

Other:
- Washable toy stuffing

Fasten off.
Allowing tail to curl as much as possible, sew end to back of body.

EARS
(Make 2)
With 4mm hook, ch 3.
ROW 1: 2tr in 3rd ch from hook, turn.
ROW 2: ch 1 (does not count as a st), 2 dc in first st, 1 dc in next st, 2 dc in last dc, turn .... (5 sts)
ROW 3: ch 3, 1tr in base of 3ch, [miss next st, 2 tr in next st] twice, turn.....(6 sts)
ROW 4: ch 1, 2 dc in first st, 1 dc in next 5 sts, turn..(7 sts)
ROW 5: ch 3, 1 tr in base of 3ch, [miss next st, 2 tr in next st] 3 times ...... (8 sts)
Fasten off.
Sew fastened-off edges to sides of head.

FLOWER
With 4mm hook, ch 6. Slst in 1st ch to form a ring.
RND 1: ch 3 (counts as 1dc and 2 ch), into ring work (1 dc, ch 2) 5 times, slst in 1st of 3ch.
RND 2: Slst in first chsp, work 1 dc, 3 tr and 1 dc in first chsp, (work 1 dc, 3tr and 1 dc in next chsp) 5 times, slst in first dc, then ch 10 for stem.
Fasten off.
Attach top of flower stem to hands.

ROSALITA THE COW

EXPAND THE FARMYARD WITH THIS ADORABLE CUDDLY COW

You Will Need...

Yarn:
- Cotton yarn suitable for your hook size. Here we have used a heavy cotton aran yarn in:
- White (130g)
- Pink (15g)
- Brown (30g)
- Black (15g)
- Beige (10g)

Tools:
- 4mm crochet hook
- Scissors
- Yarn needle
- Stitch marker
- Pins

Other:
- Fibrefill stuffing
- 2 14mm safety eyes

Pattern

* **NOTE:** This pattern is worked in continous spirals unless otherwise stated. Use a stitch marker at the end of each round.

HEAD
Using white, make a magic ring.
RND 1: 6 dc in magic ring   (6 sts)
RND 2: 2 dc in each st........................ (12 sts)
RND 3: (1 dc in next st, 2 dc in next st) 6 times.. (18 sts)
RND 4: (1 dc in next 2 sts, 2 dc in next st) 6 times... (24 sts)
RND 5: (1 dc in next 3 sts, 2 dc in next st) 6 times... (30 sts)
RND 6: (1 dc in next 4 sts, 2 dc in next st) 6 times... (36 sts)
RND 7: (1 dc in next 5 sts, 2 dc in next st) 6 times... (42 sts)
RND 8: (1 dc in next 6 sts, 2 dc in next st) 6 times... (48 sts)
RND 9: (1 dc in next 7 sts, 2 dc in next st) 6 times... (54 sts)
RND 10: (1 dc in next 8 sts, 2 dc in next st) 6 times... (60 sts)
RNDS 11-21: 1 dc in each st............. (60 sts)
Insert the safety eyes between rows 15 and 16 with a gap of 9 visible stitches.
RND 22: (1 dc in next 8 sts, dc2tog) 6 times.. (54 sts)
RND 23: (1 dc in next 7 sts, dc2tog) 6 times.. (48 sts)
RND 24: (1 dc in next 6 sts, dc2tog) 6 times.. (42 sts)
RND 25: (1 dc in next 5 sts, dc2tog) 6 times.. (36 sts)
RND 26: (1 dc in next 4 sts, dc2tog) 6 times.. (30 sts)
RND 27: (1 dc in next 3 sts, dc2tog) 6 times.. (24 sts)
Fasten off and weave in all loose ends. Stuff the head.

BODY
Using white, make a magic ring.
RND 1: 6 dc in magic ring................... (6 sts)
RND 2: 2 dc in each st........................ (12 sts)
RND 3: (1 dc in next st, 2 dc in next st) 6 times.. (18 sts)
RND 4: (1 dc in next 2 sts, 2 dc in next st) 6 times... (24 sts)
RND 5: (1 dc in next 3 sts, 2 dc in next st) 6

Tip

Why not size up your yarn and hook to make a jumbo-sized Rosalita?

times ....(30 sts)
RND 6: (1 dc in next 4 sts, 2 dc in next st) 6
times ....(36 sts)
RND 7: (1 dc in next 5 sts, 2 dc in next st) 6
times ....(42 sts)
RND 8: (1 dc in next 6 sts, 2 dc in next st) 6
times ....(48 sts)
RND 9: (1 dc in next 7 sts, 2 dc in next st) 6
times ....(54 sts)
RNDS 10-19: 1 dc in each st ....(54 sts)
RND 20: (1 dc in next 7 sts, dc2tog)
6 times..(48 sts)
RND 21: 1 dc in each st.....................(48 sts)
RND 22: (1 dc in next 6 sts, dc2tog)
6 times..(42 sts)
RND 23: 1 dc in each st ....(42 sts)
RND 24: (1 dc in next 5 sts, dc2tog)
6 times..(36 sts)

RND 25: 1 dc in each st ....(36 sts)
RND 26: (1 dc in next 4 sts, dc2tog)
6 times..(30 sts)
RND 27: 1 dc in each st.....................(30 sts)
RND 28: (1 dc in next 3 sts, dc2tog)
6 times..(24 sts)
RND 29: 1 dc in each st ....(24 sts)
Fasten off, leaving long tail for
assembly. Stuff the body with filling.

Pin and sew head to body, adding more
stuffing to support neck.

NOSE

Using pink, ch 9.
You will be crocheting around the
foundation chain.
RND 1: Starting in 2nd ch from hook, 1 dc

in next 7 chs, 4 dc in last ch for the corner, 1 dc in next 6 chs, 3 dc in next st ....
....(20 sts)
RND 2: 2 dc in next st, 1 dc in next 7 sts, 2 dc in next st, 1 dc in next st, 2 dc in next st, 1 dc in next 7 sts, 2 dc in next st, 1 dc in next st.. (24 sts)
RND 3: 2 dc in next st, 1 dc in next 9 sts, 2 dc in next st, 1 dc in next st, 2 dc in next st, 1 dc in next 11 sts, 2 dc in next st, 1 dc in next st.. (28 sts)
RND 4: 2 dc in next st, 1 dc in next 11 sts, 2 dc in next st, 1 dc in next st, 2 dc in next st, 1 dc in next 11 sts, 2 dc in next st, 1 dc in next st.. (32 sts)
RND 5: 2 dc in next st, 1 dc in next 13 sts, 2 dc in next st, 1 dc in next st, 2 dc in next st, 1 dc in next 13 sts, 2 dc in next st, 1 dc in next st.. (36 sts)
RND 6: (1 dc in next 5 sts, 2 dc in next st) 6 times.. (42 sts)
RNDS 7-9: 1 dc in each st.................. (42 sts)
RND 10: (1 dc in next 5 sts, dc2tog) 6 times.. (36 sts)
Fasten off, leaving long tail for assembly. Stuff the nose with filling.

Pin and sew on the nose onto the cow's

head one stitch under the eyes between rows 18 and 25 on the head.

ARMS
(Make 2)
Using brown, make a magic ring.
RND 1: 6 dc in magic ring.................... (6 sts)
RND 2: 2 dc in each st........................ (12 sts)
RND 3: (1 dc in next st, 2 dc in next st) 6 times.. (18 sts)
RND 4: 1 dc in BLO of each st........... (18 sts)
RNDS 5-8: 1 dc in each st .... (18 sts)
Change to white yarn.
RNDS 9-10: 1 dc in each st................ (18 sts)
RND 11: (1 dc in next 4 sts, dc2tog) 3 times.. (15 sts)
RNDS 12-24: 1 dc in each st .... (15 sts)
RND 25: (1 dc in next 3 sts, dc2tog) 3 times.. (12 sts)
Finish off, leaving long tail for assembly.

Pin and sew arms to body, stuffing the arms with filling.

LEGS
(Make 2)
Using brown, make a magic ring.
RND 1: 6 dc in magic ring.................... (6 sts)

RND 2: 2 dc in each st........................ (12 sts)
RND 3: (1 dc in next st, 2 dc in next st) 6 times.. (18 sts)
RND 4: (1 dc in next 2 sts, 2 dc in next st) 6 times.. (24 sts)
RND 5: 1 dc in BLO of each st .... (24 sts)
RNDS 6-8: 1 dc in each st .... (24 sts)
Change to white yarn.
RNDS 9-10: 1 dc in each st .... (24 sts)
RND 11: (1 dc in next 4 sts, dc2tog) 4 times.. (20 sts)
RNDS 12-13: 1 dc in each st............. (20 sts)
RND 14: (1 dc in next 3 sts, dc2tog) 4 times.. (16 sts)
RNDS 15-16: 1 dc in each st .... (16 sts)
RND 17: (1 dc in next 2 sts, dc2tog) 4 times.. (12 sts)
RNDS 18-20: 1 dc in each st........... (12 sts)
Stuff the legs with filling. Fasten off, leaving long tail for assembly.

Pin and sew legs to body as shown.

HORNS
(Make 2)
Using beige, make a magic ring.
RND 1: 6 dc in magic ring.................... (6 sts)
RND 2: (1 dc in next st, 2 dc in next st)

3 times.......................................(9 sts)
RND 3: 1 dc in each st.........................(9 sts)
RND 4: (1 dc in next 2 sts, 2 dc in next st) 3 times......................................(12 sts)
RND 5: 1 dc in each st.......................(12 sts)
RND 6: (1 dc in next 3 sts, 2 dc in next st) 3 times......................................(15 sts)
RND 7: 1 dc in each st.......................(15 sts)
Fasten off, leaving long tail for assembly.

Pin and sew horns between row 7 and 11 on the head.

EARS
(Make 2)
Make 1 ear in brown and the other in beige.
Using your chosen colour, make a magic ring.
RND 1: 6 dc in magic ring...................(6 sts)
RND 2: (1 dc in next st, 2 dc in next st) 3 times..(9 sts)
RND 3: (1 dc in next 2 sts, 2 dc in next st) 3 times......................................(12 sts)
RND 4: 1 dc in each st.......................(12 sts)
RND 5: (1 dc in next st, 2 dc in next st) 6 times......................................(18 sts)
RNDS 6-9: 1 dc in each st ....(18 sts)
RND 10: (1 dc in next st, dc2tog) 6 times....
....(12 sts)
RND 11: 1 dc in each st.....................(12 sts)
Fasten off, leaving long tail for assembly.

Pin and sew the ears in place just under the horns on the side of the head.

TAIL
Using brown, make a magic ring.
RND 1: 6 dc in magic ring.................(6 sts)
RND 2: (1 dc in next st, 2 dc in next st) 3 times..(9 sts)
RND 3: 1 dc in each st.........................(9 sts)
RND 4: (1 dc in next 2 sts, 2 dc in next st) 3 times......................................(12 sts)
RND 5: (1 dc in next 3 sts, 2 dc in next st) 3 times......................................(15 sts)
RND 6: (1 dc in next 4 sts, 2 dc in next st) 3 times......................................(18 sts)
RNDS 7-8: 1 dc in each st..................(18 sts)
RND 9: (1 dc in next st, dc2tog) 6 times......
....(12 sts)
RND 10: (1 dc in next 2 sts, dc2tog) 3 times......................................(9 sts)

Change to white yarn.
RNDS 11-25: 1 dc in each st ....(9 sts)
Stuff the tail with fibrefill. Fasten off, leaving long tail for assembly.

Pin and sew on the tail between rows 13 and 14 on the back of the body.

BIG DOTS
(Make 2)
Using black, make a magic ring.
RND 1: 6 dc in magic ring...................(6 sts)
RND 2: 2 dc in each st.......................(12 sts)
RND 3: (1 dc in next st, 2 dc in next st)

6 times.......................................(18 sts)
RND 4: (1 dc in next 2 sts, 2 dc in next st) 6 times......................................(24 sts)
Fasten off, leaving long tail for assembly.

MEDIUM DOTS
(Make 2)
Using black, make a magic ring.
RND 1: 6 dc in magic ring...................(6 sts)
RND 2: 2 dc in each st.......................(12 sts)
RND 3: (1 dc in next st, 2 dc in next st) 6 times......................................(18 sts)
Fasten off, leaving long tail for assembly.

SMALL DOTS
(Make 2)
Using black, make a magic ring.
RND 1: 6 dc in magic ring...................(6 sts)
RND 2: 2 dc in each st.......................(12 sts)
Fasten off, leaving long tail for assembly.

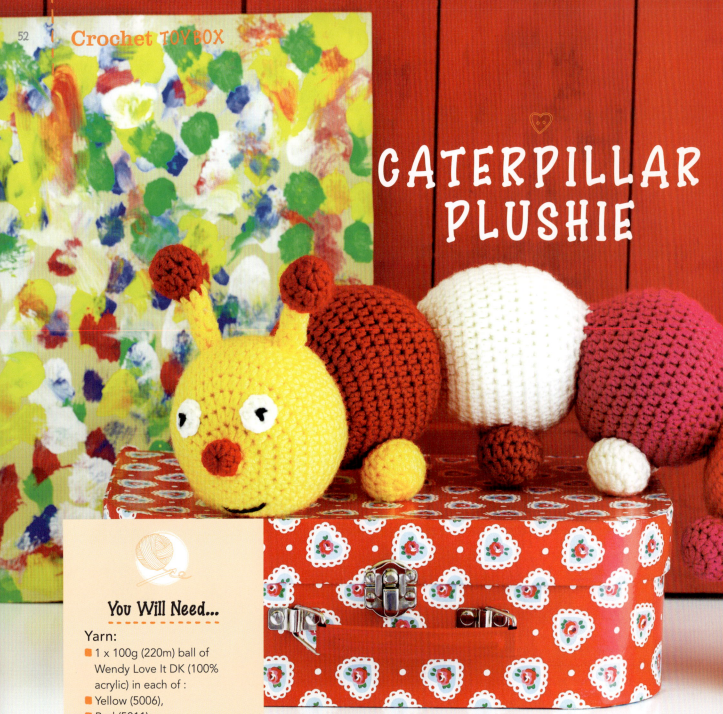

CATERPILLAR PLUSHIE

You Will Need...

Yarn:
- 1 x 100g (220m) ball of Wendy Love It DK (100% acrylic) in each of :
- Yellow (5006),
- Red (5011),
- Cream (5002),
- Fuchsia (5010),
- Orange (5008)
- Purple (5009)*.
- Length of Black DK yarn for embroidery.

Tools:
- 3.5mm hook (US E-4)

Other:
- Washable toy stuffing

THIS LOVELY LONG CATERPILLAR IS THE PERFECT ADDITION TO ANY CHILD'S BEDROOM

Pattern

Finished product size: approx. 55cm/21½in long

* **HALF TREBLE CROCHET DECREASE (HTR2TOG):** work 2htr together thus: (yarn round hook, insert hook in next st, yarn round hook and pull through) twice, yarn round hook and pull through all 5 loops on hook.

* **NOTE:** Yarn amounts are based on average requirements and are therefore approx. Instructions in brackets are worked as stated after 2nd bracket.

HEAD

RND 1: With 3.5mm and Yellow, make slip ring as follows: wind yarn round index finger of left hand to form ring, insert hook into ring, yarn over hook and pull through, ch 1 (does not count as st), work 8htr in ring, pull end of yarn tightly to close ring.
Mark end of last round and move marker up at end of every round.
RND 2: 2 htr in each st .... (16 sts)
RND 3: (2 htr in next st, 1 htr in next st)

8 times..(24 sts)
RND 4: (2 htr in next st, 1 htr in next 2 sts) 8 times ....(32 sts)
RND 5: (2 htr in next st, 1 htr in next 3 sts) 8 times ....40 sts.
RND 6: (2 htr in next st, 1 htr in next 4 sts) 8 times ....(48 sts)
RND 7-12: 1 htr in each st ....(48 sts)
RND 13: (1 htr in next 4 sts, htr2tog) 8 times..(40 sts)
RND 14: (1 htr in next 3 sts, htr2tog) 8 times..(32 sts)
RND 15: (1 htr in next 2 sts, htr2tog) 8 times..(24 sts)
RND 16: (1 htr in next st, htr2tog) 8 times.. (16 sts)
Fasten off.

Stuff head firmly.

BODY

First segment: Join Red and work rnds 3-16. Fasten off.
Stuff segment firmly.
Second segment: Join Cream and work rnds 3-16. Fasten off.
Stuff segment firmly.
Third segment: Join Fuchsia and work rnds 3-16. Fasten off.
Stuff segment firmly.
Fourth segment: Join Orange and work rnds 3-16. Fasten off.
Stuff segment firmly.
Fifth segment: Join Purple and work rnds 3-16. Fasten off.
Stuff segment firmly.
RND 17: htr2tog 8 times ....(8 sts)
Fasten off.

Gather last round, pull up tightly and secure.

FEET

RND 1: With 3.5mm hook and Yellow, make slip ring as on head, ch 1 (does not count as st), work 8 htr in ring, pull end of yarn tightly to close ring.
Mark end of last round and move marker up at end of every round.
RND 2: 2 htr in each s .... (16 sts)
RNDS 3-4: 1 htr in each st .... (16 sts)
Stuff foot firmly.

RND 5: htr2tog 8 times.................(8 sts)
Fasten off.
Make 1 more foot in Yellow. Sew fastened-off edge of feet to Red segment of body.

Make a pair of feet in Red and sew to Cream segment of body.

Make a pair of feet in Cream and sew to Fuchsia segment of body.

Make a pair of feet in Fuchsia and sew to Orange segment of body.

Make a pair of feet in Orange and sew to Purple segment of body.

ANTENNA
(Make 2)
RND 1: With 3.5mm hook and Red, make slip ring as on head, ch 1 (does not count as st), work 8 htr in ring, pull end of yarn tightly to close ring.
Mark end of last round and move marker up at end of every round.
RND 2: (2 htr in next st, 1 htr in next st) 4 times.. (12 sts)
RND 3: 1htr in each st .... (12 sts)
Stuff antenna firmly, adding stuffing as you work.
RND 4: htr2tog 6 times.................(6 sts)
Join in Yellow.
RNDS 5-8: 1 htr in each st ....(6 sts)
Slst in first st. Fasten off.

Sew fastened-off edge to top of head.

NOSE

RND 1: With 3.5mm hook and Red, make slip ring as on head, ch 1 (does not count as st), work 8 htr in ring, pull end of yarn tightly to close ring.
RND 2: 1 htr in each st, slst in first st.
Fasten off.

Stuff firmly. Sew fastened-off edge to front of face.

EYES
(Make 2)
RND 1: With 3.5mm hook and Cream, make slip ring as on head, ch 1 (does not count as st), work 8htr in ring, pull end of yarn tightly to close ring, slst in first st.
Fasten off.

Sew to front of head.

With Black, embroider pupil on each eye, then work long straight stitch on head below nose for mouth.

FOX PUPPET

THIS PLAYFUL AND CUTE CROCHET PUPPET WILL MELT ANY LITTLE ONE'S HEART

Pattern by:

Sascha Blase - van Wagtendonk

Sascha Blase is a Dutch pattern designer known as 'A la Sascha'. She has written ten Dutch crochet books and is currently working on her eleventh. Her bestseller, Crochet Ragdolls, is now available in English.

@alasascha

You Will Need...

Yarn:
- Chunky yarn in your chosen colours. Here we have used Durable Cosy in:
- Colour 1: Brown (1 ball)
- Colour 2: Orange (2 balls)
- Colour 3: White (1 ball)

Tools:
- 5mm hook (US H/8)
- Yarn needle

Other:
- Fibrefill stuffing
- 15mm gold and black safety eyes

Pattern

Finished product size: 24cm (9in) long (excluding tail),12cm (5in) wide

* **TENSION:** Tension is not critical
* **NOTES:** 1.Most pieces are worked in a spiral, in continuous rounds. Using a stitch marker in the first stitch of each round is the easiest way to keep track of the start of each round. 2.The neatest way to change colour is to complete the last step of previous stitch with the new colour, for example: if the last stitch before the change is a dc, the last yarn over hook and pull through 2 loops will be with the new colour.

PUPPET BASE

With col 1, start with a magic ring.
RND 1 (RS): Ch 1, work 6 dc into the ring...(6 sts)
RND 2: 2 dc in each st......................(12 sts)
RND 3: (1 dc in next st, 2 dc in next) 3 times, 1 dc in next st, change to col 2, 2 dc in next st, change to col 3, (1 dc in next st, 2 dc in next st) twice ....(18 sts)
Fasten off col 1.

RND 4: (1 dc in next 2 sts, 2 dc in next st) 3 times, 1 dc in next st, change to col 2, 1 dc in next st, 2 dc in next, 1 dc in next st, change to col 3, 1 dc in next st, 2 dc in next, 1 dc in next 2 sts, 2 dc in next st. ....
....(24 sts)
RND 5: (1 dc in next 3 sts, 2 dc in next st) 3 times, 1 dc in next st, change to col 2, 1 dc in next 2 sts, 2 dc in next, 1 dc in next 2 sts, change to col 3, 1 dc in next st, 2 dc in next, 1 dc in next 3 sts, 2 dc in next st ... (30 sts)
RND 6: (1 dc in next 4 sts, 2 dc in next st) 3 times, 1 dc in next st, change to col 2, 1 dc in next 3 sts, 2 dc in next st, 1 dc in next 3 sts, change to col 3, 1 dc in next st, 2 dc in next st, 1 dc in next 4 sts, 2 dc in next st...(36 sts)
RND 7: 1 dc in next 19 sts, change to col 2, 1 dc in next 9 sts, change to col 3, 1 dc in next 8 sts ....(36 sts)
RND 8: 1 dc in next 19 sts, change to col 2, 1 dc in next 10 sts, change to col 3, 1 dc in next 7 sts ....(36 sts)
RND 9: 1 dc in next 19 sts, change to col 2, 1 dc in next 11 sts, change to col 3, 1 dc in next 6 sts ....(36 sts)
RND 10: 1 dc in next 19 sts, change to col 2, 1 dc in next 12 sts, change to col 3, 1 dc in next 5 sts...(36 sts)
RND 11: 1 dc in next 19 sts, change to col 2, 1 dc in next 17 sts ....(36 sts)
Fasten off col 3.

RNDS 12–19: 1 dc in each st..............(36 sts)
RND 20: 1 dc in next 2 sts, ch 12, sk next 12 sts (for mouth), 1 dc in next 22 st ....
....(36 sts)
RND 21: 1 dc in each st and ch ....(36 sts)
RNDS 22–40: 1 dc in each st.............(36 sts)
Fasten off and weave in ends.

MOUTH

RND 1: With col 2, starting at first skipped stitch of rnd 20, 1 dc in each skipped st and in each ch of rnd 20. ....
....(24 sts)
RNDS 2-9: 1 dc in each st ....(24 sts)
RND 10: Change to col 3, 1 dc in ➡

each st ....(24 sts)
Fasten off col 2.

RND 11: (1 dc in next 4 sts, dc2tog) to end.
(20 sts)
RND 12: (1 dc in next 3 sts, dc2tog) to end
(16 sts)
RND 13: (1 dc in next 2 sts, dc2tog) to end
(12 sts)
RND 14: (1 dc in next st, dc2tog) to end .....
(8 sts)
Cut yarn and fasten off. Weave through
8 remaining stitches and pull tight to
close the gap; weave in ends.

EARS
(Make 02)
RND 1 (RS): With col 1, ch 1, work 6dc in the
ring...(6 sts)
RND 2: (1 dc in next st, 2 dc in next st) to
end..(9 sts)
RND 3: Change to col 2, 1 dc in each st. ....
....(9 sts)
Fasten off col 1.

RND 4: (1 dc in next 2 sts, 2 dc in next st) to
end..(12 sts)
RND 5: 1 dc in each st........................(12 sts)
RND 6: (1 dc in next 3 sts, 2 dc in next st) to

end...(15 sts)
RND 7: 1 dc in each st........................(15 sts)
RND 8: (1 dc in next 4 sts, 2 dc in next st) to
end...(18 sts)
RND 9: 1 dc in each st........................(18 sts)
Fasten off, leaving a long tail to attach
ears on each side of the head between
rnds 17-18, 4 stitches apart. It's easiest
to determine exact placement when
folded flat and placed on a surface.

Take the safety eyes and insert them
between rnds 12-13 on each side of the
head, 7 stitches apart.

TAIL
With col 3, start with a magic ring.
RND 1 (RS): Ch 1, work 6 dc into the ring.
....(6 sts)
RND 2: (1 dc in next st, 2 dc in next st) to
end..(9 sts)
RND 3: 1 dc in each st..........................(9 sts)
RND 4: (1 dc in next 2 sts, 2 dc in next st) to
end..(12 sts)
RND 5: 1 dc in each st........................(12 sts)
RND 6: (1 dc in next 3 sts, 2 dc in next st) to
end..(15 sts)
RND 7: Change to col 2, 1dc in each st.
....(15 sts)
Fasten off col 3.
RND 8: (1 dc in next 4 sts, 2 dc in next st) to
end...(18 sts)
RND 9: (1 dc in next 5 sts, 2 dc in next st) to
end...(21 sts)
RNDS 10–12: 1 dc in each st ....(21 sts)
RND 13: (1 dc in next 5 sts, dc2tog) to
end...(18 sts)
RND 14: 1 dc in each st......................(18 sts)
RND 15: (1 dc in next 4 sts, dc2tog) to end.
(15 sts)
RND 16: 1 dc in each st......................(15 sts)
RND 17: (1 dc in next 3 sts, dc2tog) to
end...(12 sts)
RND 18: 1 dc in each st......................(12 sts)
Stuff the tail lightly with fibrefill.

RND 19: dc2tog to end ....(6 sts)
Fasten off and weave yarn through 6
remaining stitches and pull tight to
close the gap but leave a long yarn tail,
to attach tail in the center of the base
between rnds 36-38.

"There is something rather charming about this little woodland creature"

THE ALPACA FAMILY

Pattern by:

Lucy Collin

Lucy learned to crochet when she was a child, but started making crochet toys when she had children of her own. She has been designing patterns to make cute and unusual creatures and characters for ten years, and has had several books published including Star Wars and Harry Potter crochet books.

www.lucyravenscar.etsy.com

You Will Need...

Yarn:
- You will need to use DK weight yarn in your chosen colours. We have used Stylecraft Alpaca DK in:
- Orchid or Teal for adult alpaca (70g)
- Lime for baby alpaca (50g)
- Toffee or Cream (10g)
- Small amount of black yarn to sew features

Tools:
- 3.5mm hook (US E/4)
- Stitch marker
- Yarn needle

Other:
- Fibrefill stuffing
- Two 10.5mm black safety eyes for each alpaca

CREATE THIS ADORABLE GROUP OF WOOLLY ALPACAS

Pattern

Finished product size: Adult: 21cm (8¼in) tall
Baby: 17cm (6¾in) tall

* **SPECIAL STITCHES:** dc2tog: double crochet 2 sts together as follows: insert hook into next st, yoh and pull a loop through (2 loops on hook), insert hook into next st, yoh and pull a loop through (3 loops on hook), yoh and pull through all 3 loops
* **NOTES:** Most pieces are worked in a spiral, without joining each round. It may help to use a stitch marker to mark the first stitch of the round and then move it up as you work each round.

ADULT ALPACA FACE
Using col 2, ch 2.
RND 1: 6 dc in 2nd ch from hook.... (6 sts)
RND 2: 2 dc in each st .... (12 sts)
RND 3: 1 dc in each st. ....(12 sts)
RND 4: (2 dc in next st, 1 dc in next st) 6 times............................... (18 sts)
RND 5: 1 dc in each st. .... (18 sts)
RND 6: 1 dc in next 3 sts, (2 dc in next st) 3 times, 1 dc in next 6 sts, (2 dc in next st) 3 times, dc in next 3 sts .... (24 sts)
RND 7: 1 dc in each st .... (24 sts)
RND 8: 1 dc in next 5 sts, (2 dc in next st) 3 times, 1 dc in next 9 sts, (2 dc in next st) 3 times, 1 dc in next 4 st............ .... (30 sts)
RND 9: 1 dc in next 5 sts, (2 dc in next st, 1 dc in next st) 3 times, 1 dc in next 9 sts, (2 dc in next st, 1 dc in next st) 3 times, dc in next 4 sts .... (36 sts)
RND 10: (2 dc in next st, 1 dc in next 5 sts) 6 times .... (42 sts)
RND 11: 1 dc in each st .... (42 sts)
Sl st in next st and fasten off, leaving a tail for sewing.

HEAD AND NECK
Using col 1, ch 2.
RND 1: 6 dc in 2nd ch from hook .... (6 sts)
RND 2: 2 dc in each st ....(12 sts)

RND 3: (2 dc in next st, 1 dc in next st) 6 times............................... (18 sts)
RND 4: (2 dc in next st, 1 dc in next 2 sts) 6 times .... (24 sts)
RND 5: (2 dc in next st, 1 dc in next 3 sts) 6 times. .... (30 sts)
RND 6: (2 dc in next st, 1 dc in next 4 sts) 6 times. .... (36 sts)
RND 7: (2 dc in next st, 1 dc in next 5 sts) 6 times. .... (42 sts)
RND 8: (2 dc in next st, 1 dc in next 6 sts) 6 times. .... (48 sts)
RND 9: (2 dc in next st, 1 dc in next 7 sts) 6 times. .... (54 sts)
RNDS 10-20: 1 dc in each st...... (54 sts)
RND 21: (dc2tog, 1 dc in next 7 sts) 6 times... (48 sts)
RND 22: (dc2tog, 1 dc in next 6 sts) 6 times... (42 sts)
To fix face to head: arrange face with the start of the round at the bottom and push eyes between

RNDS 8 and 9. Then push eyes through head between RNDS 15 and 16.

Secure backs of eyes with washers.
RND 23: (dc2tog, 1 dc in next 5 sts) 6 times... (36 sts)
RND 24: (dc2tog, 1 dc in next 4 sts) 6 times... (30 sts)
RNDS 25-34: 1 dc in each st...... (30 sts)

Sl st in next st and fasten off, leaving a tail for sewing.

BODY

RNDS 1-7: Using col 1, work as given for head and neck to end of rnd 7 .... (42 sts)

RNDS 8-33: 1 dc in each st. (42 sts) Stuff body as far as you can and continue stuffing as you go along.

RND 34: (dc2tog, 1 dc in next 5 sts) 6 times .... (36 sts)

RND 35: (dc2tog, 1 dc in next 4 sts) 6 times. .... (30 sts)

RND 36: (dc2tog, 1 dc in next 3 sts) 6 times. .... (24 sts)

RND 37: (dc2tog, 1 dc in next 2 sts) 6 times .... (18 sts)

RND 38: (dc2tog, 1 dc in next st) 6 times.............................. (12 sts)

RND 39: (dc2tog) 6 times .... (6 sts) Fasten off, leaving a length of yarn.

Finish stuffing firmly and sew hole shut neatly.

EARS

(Make 2)

Using col 2, ch 2.

RND 1: 6 dc in 2nd ch from hook.......... .... (6 sts)

RND 2: 1 dc in each st .... (6 sts)

RND 3: (2 dc in next st, 1 dc in next 2 sts) twice .... (8 sts)

RND 4: 1 dc in each st .... (8 sts)

RND 5: (2 dc in next st, 1 dc in next 3 sts) twice .... (10 sts)

RND 6: 1 dc in each st .... (10 sts)

RND 7: (2 dc in next st, 1 dc in next 4 sts) twice .... (12 sts)

RNDS 8-9: 1 dc in each st............(12 sts) Sl st in next st and fasten off, leaving a length of yarn.

LEGS

(Make 4)

Using col 1, ch2.

RND 1: 6 dc in 2nd ch from hook.......... .... (6 sts)

RND 2: 2 dc in each st .... (12 sts)

RND 3: (2 dc in next st, 1 dc in next 3 sts) 3 times .... (15 sts)

RNDS 4-17: 1 dc in each st ....(15 sts) Sl st in next st and fasten off, leaving a length of yarn.

TAIL

Using col 1, ch 2.

RND 1: 6 dc in 2nd ch from hook.......... .... (6 sts)

RND 2: (2 dc in next st, 1 dc in next st) 3 times............................... (9 sts)

RND 3: (2 dc in next st, 1 dc in next 2 sts) 3 times .... (12 sts)

RND 4: (2 dc in next st, 1 dc in next 3 sts) 3 times .... (15 sts)

RNDS 5-8: 1 dc in each st............(15 sts)

RND 9: (dc2tog, 1 dc in next 3 sts) 3 times............................... (12 sts)

RNDS 10-11: 1 dc in each st .... (12 sts) Sl st in next st and fasten off, leaving a length of yarn.

BABY ALPACA FACE

Using col 2, ch 2.

RND 1: 6 dc in 2nd ch from hook.......... .... (6 sts)

RND 2: 2 dc in each st .... (12 sts)

RND 3: 1 dc in each st .... (12 sts)

RND 4: (2 dc in next st, 1 dc in next st) 6 times... (18 sts)

RND 5: 1 dc in next 3 sts, (2 dc in next st) 3 times, 1 dc in next 6 sts, (2 dc in next st) 3 times, 1 dc in next 3 sts. .... (24 sts)

RND 6: 1 dc in next 3 sts, (2 dc in next st, 1 dc in next st) 3 times, 1 dc in next 6 sts, (2 dc in next st, 1 dc in next st) 3 times, 1 dc in next 3 sts. .... (30 sts)

RND 7: 1 dc in next 7 sts, 2 dc in next st, 1 dc in next 6 sts, 2 dc in next st, 1 dc in next 6 sts, 2 dc in next st, 1 dc in next 8 sts .... (33 sts)

RND 8: 1 dc in each st .... (33 sts) Sl st in next st and fasten off, leaving a length of yarn.

HEAD AND NECK

Using col 1, ch 2.

RND 1: 6 dc in 2nd ch from hook........... .... (6 sts)

RND 2: 2 dc in each st .... (12 sts)

RND 3: (2 dc in next st, 1 dc in next st) 6 times... (18 sts)

RND 4: (2 dc in next st, 1 dc in next 2

sts) 6 times. .... (24 sts)

RND 5: (2 dc in next st, 1 dc in next 3 sts) 6 times. .... (30 sts)

RND 6: (2 dc in next st, 1 dc in next 4 sts) 6 times. .... (36 sts)

RND 7: (2 dc in next st, 1 dc in next 5 sts) 6 times. .... (42 sts)

RND 8: (2 dc in next st, 1 dc in next 13 sts) 3 times. .... (45 sts)

RNDS 9-16: 1 dc in each st. .... (45 sts)

RND 17: (dc2tog, 1 dc in next 13 sts) 3 times... (42 sts)

RND 18: (dc2tog, 1 dc in next 5 sts) 6 times... (36 sts)

To fix face to head: arrange face with the start of the round at the bottom and push eyes between rnds 6 and 7. Then push eyes through head between rnds 12 and 13. Secure backs of eyes with washers.

RND 19: (dc2tog, 1 dc in next 4 sts) 6 times... . (30 sts)

RND 20: (dc2tog, 1 dc in next 3 sts) 6 times... (24 sts)

RNDS 21-29: 1 dc in each st around .... (24 sts)

Sl st in next st and fasten off, leaving a length of yarn.

BODY

RNDS 1-5: Using col 1, work as given for head and neck to end of rnd 5. .... (30 sts).

RND 6: (2 dc in next st, 1 dc in next 9 sts) 3 times. .... (33 sts)

RNDS 7-24: 1 dc in each st .... (33 sts)
Stuff body as far as you can and continue stuffing as you go along.

RND 25: (dc2tog, 1 dc in next 9 sts) 3 times....................................... (30 sts)

RND 26: (dc2tog, 1 dc in next 3 sts) 6 times... (24 sts)

RND 27: (dc2tog, 1 dc in next 2 sts) 6 times... (18 sts)

RND 28: (dc2tog, 1 dc in next st) 6 times.. (12 sts)

RND 29: (dc2tog) 6 times .... (6 sts)
Fasten off, leaving a length of yarn.

Finish stuffing firmly and sew hole shut neatly.

EARS

(Make 2)

RNDS 1-5: Using col 2, work as given for adult alpaca ears to end of rnd 5. ....(10 sts)

RNDS 6-8: 1 dc in each st. ....(10 sts)

Sl st in next st and fasten off, leaving a length of yarn.

LEGS

(Make 4)

Using col 1 ch 2.

RND 1: 5 dc in 2nd ch from hook. .... (5 sts)

RND 2: 2 dc in each st. .... (10 sts)

RNDS 3-14: 1 dc in each st. .... (10 sts)
Sl st in next st and fasten off, leaving a tail of yarn.

TAIL

Using col 1, ch 2.

RND 1: 6 dc in 2nd ch from hook .... (6 sts)

RND 2: (2 dc in next st, 1 dc in next st) 3 times... (9 sts)

RND 3: (2 dc in next st, 1 dc in next 2 sts) 3 times. ....(12 sts)

RNDS 4-6: 1 dc in each st........... (12 sts)

RND 7: (dc2tog, 1 dc in next 2 sts) 3 times.. (9 sts)

RND 8: 1 dc in each st .... (9 sts)
Sl st in next st and fasten off, leaving a length of yarn.

PUTTING TOGETHER BOTH ALPACAS

1 Stuff head and neck firmly, then sew them to the body.

2 Using black yarn, embroider nose and mouth onto face. Start in the centre hole then sew two lines across the first two rounds slightly up and to the left, then the same up and to the right to make the nose. Sew one line straight downwards from the centre hole over two rounds then sew a line to the left and up a little over the first three rounds. Do a matching line to the right to complete the mouth.

3 Stuff face a little then secure it to the head by sewing around the edge of the face with the length of yarn attached.

4 Sew the edges of ears together then sew to top of the head. Stuff legs firmly and sew to body. Stuff tail very lightly then sew edges together and sew in place.

5 To make the fringe of hair on the head, you will sew loops into rnds 1-3 on the top of the head, in front of the ears. Take a length of col 1 and thread it onto your needle. Sew the yarn through the head, leaving a length of yarn long enough to go over the top of the face sticking out. Then sew a stitch in the same place, taking the yarn through the stitch in a little knot to make it secure. Sew a large loop next to this, again big enough to hang down over the top of the face, then sew a securing stitch in the same place, as you did before. Continue doing this in the area in front of the ears until you have made about 16-17 loops. You can use more than one length of yarn if necessary.

6 Cut each loop and trim to length. The strands will unravel a little naturally to create a fluffy effect, but you can speed this up. Take the point of the needle through each strand to separate it or use a wire pet brush to brush the fringe.

You Will Need...

Yarn:
- You will need to use 4 ply weight cotton yarn. Here we have used:
- Colour 1: Red (30yds)
- Colour 2: Orange (50yds)
- Colour 3: Yellow (80yds)
- Colour 4: Green (120yds)
- Colour 5: Light Blue (120yds)
- Colour 6: Dark Blue (140yds)
- Colour 7: Purple (160yds)
- Colour 8: Light Brown (240yds)
- Colour 9: White (10yds)
- Colour 10: Black (10yds)

Tools:
- 2mm hook
- Scissors
- Yarn needle

Other:
- Fibrefill
- Buttons
- Velcro tape

Optional
- Squeakers, bells, rattles, buttons, beads etc. to put inside the toy

MONTESSORI TURTLE

IF COLOUR IS WHAT YOU'RE AFTER, THIS TURTLE HAS THE WHOLE RAINBOW IN ITS SHELL

Pattern

* **NOTES:** All parts of the turtle - front legs, hind legs, tail, head, belly - are crocheted in a spiral, which means that the stitches are not joined at the end of each round. Use a stitch marker to mark the end of each round.
* This toy is recommended for children aged 3 and up.

FRONT LEGS
(Make 2)
Using col 8, make magic ring.
RND 1: 6 dc in magic ring.................... (6 sts)
RND 2: 2 dc in each st........................ (12 sts)
RND 3: (1 dc in next st, 2 dc in next st) 6 times.. (18 sts)
RND 4: (1 dc in next 2 sts, 2 dc in next st) 6 times.. (24 sts)
RND 5: (1 dc in next 3 sts, 2 dc in next st) 6 times.. (30 sts)
RNDS 6-8: 1 dc in each st .... (30 sts)
RND 9: dc2tog twice, 1 dc in next 11 sts, dc2tog twice, 1 dc in next 11 sts........ (26 sts)
RNDS 10-15: 1 dc in each st .... (26 sts)
Stuff with fibrefill.
Close the top and using dc across.

HIND LEGS
(Make 2)
Using col 8, make magic ring.
RND 1: 6 dc in magic ring.................... (6 sts)
RND 2: 2 dc in each st........................ (12 sts)

RND 3: (1 dc in next st, 2 dc in next st) 6 times.. (18 sts)
RND 4: (1 dc in next 2 sts, 2 dc in next st) 6 times.. (24 sts)
RND 5: (1 dc in next 3 sts, 2 dc in next st) 6 times.. (30 sts)
RNDS 6-8: 1 dc in each st .... (30 sts)
RND 9: dc2tog twice, 1 dc in next 11 sts, dc2tog twice, 1 dc in next 11 sts........ (26 sts)
RNDS 10-12: 1 dc in each st .... (26 sts)
Stuff with fibrefill.
Close the top and using dc across.

TURTLE HEAD
Using col 8, make magic ring.
RND 1: 6 dc in magic ring.................... (6 sts)
RND 2: 2 dc in each st........................ (12 sts)
RND 3: (1 dc in next st, 2 dc in next st) 6 times.. 18 sts
RND 4: (1 dc in next 2 sts, 2 dc in next st) 6 times.. (24 sts)
RND 5: (1 dc in next 3 sts, 2 dc in next st) 6 times.. (30 sts
RND 6: (1 dc in next 4 sts, 2 dc in next st) 6 times.. (36 sts
RNDS 7-11: 1 dc in each st .... (36 sts)
RND 12: (1 dc in next 4 sts, dc2tog) 6 times (30 sts)
RND 13: (1 dc in next 3 sts, dc2tog) 6 times (24 sts)
RNDS 14-23: 1 dc in each st............. (24 sts)
Stuff the head, but not the neck.
Close by folding in half and using dc across.

Tip
You can use different fastenings for each coloured stripe to help your child's motor skills

TURTLE TAIL
Using col 8, make magic ring.
RND 1: 6 dc in magic ring.................... (6 sts)
RND 2: 1 dc in each st.......................... (6 sts)
RND 3: (1 dc in next st, 2 dc in next st) 3 times .... (9 sts)
RND 4: (1 dc in next 2 sts, 2 dc in next st) 3 times .... (12 sts)
RND 5: (1 dc in next 3 sts, 2 dc in next st) 3 times .... (15 sts)
RND 6: 1 dc in each st........................ (15 sts)
RND 7: (1 dc in next 4 sts, 2 dc in next st) 3 times .... (18 sts)
RND 8: (1 dc in next 8 sts, 2 dc in next st) 2 times .... (20 sts)
RNDS 9-12: 1 dc in each st............... (20 sts)
Stuff with fibrefill.
Close by folding in half and using dc across.

COLOURED STRIPES
RED
(Make 1)
Using col 1, ch 33.
ROW 1: 1 tr in 3rd ch from hook, 1 tr in each ch .... (30 sts)
Using buttons or velcro: 5 tr in last ch
Using poppers: 1 tr, ch 3 ch, 1 tr in last ch
ROW 2: 1 tr in each ch along the other side of ch .... (31 sts)
Finish off.

ORANGE
(Make 2)
Using col 2, ch 28.
ROW 1: 1 tr in 3rd chain from hook, 1 tr in each ch .... (24 sts)
Using buttons or velcro: 5 tr in last ch
Using poppers: 1 tr, ch 3 ch, 1 tr in last ch
ROW 2: 1 tr in each ch along the other side of ch .... (25 sts)
Finish off.

YELLOW
(Make 2)
Using col 3, ch 23.
ROW 1: 1 tr in 3rd chain from hook, 1 tr in each ch. .... (19 sts)
Using buttons or velcro: 5 tr in last ch
Using poppers: 1 tr, ch 3 ch, 1 tr in last ch

ROW 2: 1 tr in each ch along the other side of ch .... (20 sts)
Finish off.

GREEN
(Make 2)
Using col 4, ch 18.
ROW 1: 1 tr in 3rd chain from hook, 1 tr in each ch .... (14 sts)
Using buttons or velcro: 5 tr in last ch
Using poppers: 1 tr, ch 3 ch, 1 tr in last ch
ROW 2: 1 tr in each ch along the other side of ch .... (15 sts)
Finish off.

LIGHT BLUE
(Make 2)
Using col 5, ch 13.
ROW 1: 1 tr in 3rd chain from hook, 1 tr in each ch .... (9 sts)
Using buttons or velcro: 5 tr in last ch
Using poppers: 1 tr, ch 3 ch, 1 tr in last ch
ROW 2: 1 tr in each ch along the other side of ch .... (10 sts)
Finish off.

DARK BLUE
(Make 2)
Using col 6, ch 9.
ROW 1: 1 tr in 3rd chain from hook, 1 tr ⟹

Head and tail

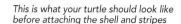

This is what your turtle should look like before attaching the shell and stripes

each ch ....(5 sts)
Using buttons or velcro: 5 tr in last ch
Using poppers: 1 tr, ch 3 ch, 1 tr in last ch
ROW 2: 1 tr in each ch along the other side
of ch ....(6 sts)
Finish off.

PURPLE
(Make 2)
Using col 7, ch 7.
ROW 1: 1 tr in 3rd chain from hook, 1 tr
each ch ....(3 sts)
Using buttons or velcro: 5 tr in last ch
Using poppers: 1 tr, ch 3 ch, 1 tr in last ch
ROW 2: 1 tr in each ch along the other side
of ch ....(4 sts)
Finish off.

TURTLE BELLY
Using col 8, make magic ring.
RND 1: 8 dc in magic ring....................(8 sts)
RND 2: 2 dc in each st....................... (16 sts)
RND 3: (1 dc in next st, 2 dc in next st) 8
times ....(24 sts)
RND 4: (1 dc in next 2 sts, 2 dc in next st) 8

times ....(32 sts)
RND 5: (1 dc in next 3 sts, 2 dc in next st) 8
times ....(40 sts)
RND 6: (1 dc in next 4 sts, 2 dc in next st) 8
times ....(48 sts)
RND 7: (1 dc in next 5 sts, 2 dc in next st) 8
times ....(56 sts)
RND 8: (1 dc in next 6 sts, 2 dc in next st) 8
times ....(64 sts)
RND 9: (1 dc in next 7 sts, 2 dc in next st) 8
times ....(72 sts)
RND 10: (1 dc in next 11 sts, 2 dc in next st)
6 times..(78 sts)
RND 11: (1 dc in next 12 sts, 2 dc in next st)
6 times..(84 sts)
RND 12: (1 dc in next 13 sts, 2 dc in next st)
6 times..(90 sts)
RND 13: (1 dc in next 14 sts, 2 dc in next st)
6 times..(96 sts)
RND 14: (1 dc in next 15 sts, 2 dc in next st)
6 times..(102 sts)
RND 15: (1 dc in next 16 sts, 2 dc in next st)
6 times..(108 sts)
RND 16: (1 dc in next 17 sts, 2 dc in next st)
6 times..(114 sts)

RND 17: (1 dc in next 18 sts, 2 dc in next st)
6 times..(120 sts)
RND 18: (1 dc in next 19 sts, 2 dc in next st)
6 times..(126 sts)
RND 19: (1 dc in next 20 sts, 2 dc in next st)

Fasteners

How you make the coloured strips will depend on your fastening method. We have provided instructions for using buttons, poppers and velcro.

The finished shell

6 times...(132 sts)
RND 20: (1 dc in next 21 sts, 2 dc in next st)
6 times...(138 sts)
RND 21: attach head using 12 dc, 1 dc in next 10 sts, attach first front leg using 13 dc, 1 dc in next 15 dc, attach first hind leg using 13 dc, 1 dc in next 7 sts, attach tail using 10 dc, 1 dc in next 7 sts, attach second hind leg using 13 dc, 1 dc in next 15 sts, attach second front long using 13 dc, 1 dc in next 10 sts...(138 sts)
Finish off and weave in ends.

COLORED TURTLE SHELL
This is worked in rounds joined at the end with a slip stitch.
Using col 1, make a magic ring.
RND 1: 6 dc in magic ring...................(6 sts)
RND 2: 2 dc in each st.......................(12 sts)
RND 3: ch 1, (1 dc in next st, 2 dc in next st) 6 times...(18 sts)
RND 4: ch 1, (1 dc in next 2 sts, 2 dc in next st)t 6 times...(24 sts)
Change to col 2.
RND 5: ch 1, (1 dc in next 3 sts, 2 dc in next

st) 6 times...(30 sts)
RND 6: ch 1, (1 dc in next 4 sts, 2 dc in next st) 6 times...(36 sts)
RND 7: ch 1, (1 dc in next 5 sts, 2 dc in next st) 6 times...(42 sts)
RND 8: ch 1, (1 dc in next 6 sts, 2 dc in next st) 6 times...(48 sts)
RND 9: ch 1, (1 dc in next 7 sts, 2 dc in next st) 6 times...(54 sts)
Change to col 3.
RND 10: ch 1, (1 dc in next 8 sts, 2 dc in next st) 6 times ....(60 sts)
RND 11: ch 1, (1 dc in next 9 sts, 2 dc in next st) 6 times ....(66 sts)
RND 12: ch 1, (1 dc in next 10 sts, 2 dc in next st) 6 times ....(72 sts)
RND 13: ch 1, (1 dc in next 11 sts, 2 dc in next st) 6 times ....(78 sts)
RND 14: ch 1, (1 dc in next 12 sts, 2 dc in next st) 6 times ....(84 sts)
Change to col 4.
RND 15: ch 1, (1 dc in next 13 sts, 2 dc in next st) 6 times ....(90 sts)
RND 16: ch 1, (1 dc in next 14 sts, 2 dc in next st) 6 times ....(96 sts)

RND 17: ch 1, (1 dc in next 15 sts, 2 dc in next st) 6 times ....(102 sts)
RND 18: ch 1, (1 dc in next 16 sts, 2 dc in next st) 6 times ....(108 sts)
RND 19: ch 1, (1 dc in next 17 sts, 2 dc in next st) 6 times ....(114 sts)
Change to col 5.
RND 20: ch 1, (1 dc in next 18 sts, 2 dc in next st) 6 times ....(120 sts)
RND 21: ch 1, (1 dc in next 19 sts, 2 dc in next st) 6 times ....(126 sts)
RND 22: ch 1, (1 dc in next 20 sts, 2 dc in next st) 6 times ....(132 sts)
RND 23: ch 1, (1 dc in next 21 sts, 2 dc in next st) 6 times ....(138 sts)
RND 24: ch 1, 1 dc in each st ....(138 sts)
Change to col 6.
RNDS 25-29: ch 1, 1 dc in each st..(138sts)
Change to col 7.
RNDS 30-34: ch 1, 1 dc in each st ....
....(138 sts)
Put shell and belly of the turtle together. You will be attaching them throughout RND 35.
RND 35: 1 dc in next 3 sts, use 6 dc to ➡

Attaching the stripes to the turtle

"If using velcro or poppers, attach one part to the end of your coloured stripes"

attach the red stripe, 1 dc in next 5 sts, use 5 dc to attach an orange stripe, 1 dc in next 5 sts, use 5 dc to attach a yellow stripe, 1 dc in next 5 sts, use 5 dc to attach a green stripe, 1 dc in next 5 sts, use 5 dc to attach a light blue stripe, 1 dc in next 5 sts, use 5 dc to attach a dark blue stripe, 1 dc in next 5 sts, use 5 dc to attach a purple stripe, 1 dc in next 12 sts.
Start stuffing.
RND 35 (CNTD): use 5 dc to attach a purple stripe, 1 dc in next 5 sts, use 5 dc to attach a dark blue stripe, 1 dc in next 5 sts, use 5 dc to attach a light blue stripe, 1 dc in next 5 sts, use 5 dc to attach a green stripe, 1 dc in next 5 sts, use 5 dc to attach a yellow stripe, 1 dc in next 5 sts, use 5 dc to attach an orange stripe, 1 dc in next 2 sts.
Finish off and weave in ends.
If using velcro or poppers, attach one part to the end of your coloured stripes.

Fold the stripes over the turtle shell to find out where to sew the other parts of the velcro or poppers, or the buttons. Sew them in place.

EYES
EYE WHITE
(Make 2)
Using col 9, make magic ring.
RND 1: 6 dc in magic ring.................... (6 sts)
RND 2: 2 dc in each st....................... (12 sts)
RND 3: (1 dc in next 3 sts, 2 dc in next st) 3 times...................................... (15 sts)
RND 4: 1 dc in each st........................ (15 sts)
Place a 10-12 mm plastic eye in the middle, or embroider the pupil with black thread.
Fasten off and weave in ends.

EYE SHELL
(Make 2)
Using col 8, make magic ring.
RND 1: 6 dc in magic ring.................... (6 sts)
RND 2: 2 dc in each st....................... (12 sts)
RND 3: (1 dc in next st, 2 dc in next st) 6 times.................................... (18 sts)
RNDS 4-5: 1 dc in each st .... (18 sts)
Fold the shell and stitch in a circle. Fasten off leaving a long tail.

Stuff eye shell and eye white, then stitch eye white to eye shell. Sew eyes to the head between rows 3 and 6. Weave in ends.

Embroider nostrils and mouth with black.

Tip

Why not change up the colours to match the playroom or bedroom?

HARRY THE HIGHLAND COW

ADD SOME SCOTTISH FLAIR TO YOUR TOYBOX

Pattern by:

Amy's Crochet Cave

Amy's Crochet Cave started in 2017 after teaching myself to crochet. I specialise in amigurumi and now have over 90 patterns published, many of which are available for free.

www.ravelry.com/designers/amys-crochet-cave

You Will Need...

Yarn:
- You will need to use DK weight yarn in your chosen colours. Here we have used Sirdar Snuggly DK in:
- Colour 1: Biscuit
- Colour 2: Rice Pudding
- Colour 3: Soft Brown

Tools:
- 3mm hook
- Yarn needle
- Stitch marker
- Scissors

Other:
- Soft toy filling
- 8mm safety eyes

Pattern

Finished product size: Approximately 24cm/9½in tall, excluding ears.

HEAD

Using col 1, ch 7.
RND 1: 1 dc in 3rd ch from hook, 1 dc in next 3 chs, 3 dc in last ch, 1 dc in back of next 4 chs, 3 dc in space between skipped chs 1 and 2 .... (14sts)
RND 2: 1 dc in next 4 sts, 2 dc in next 3 sts, 1 dc in next 4 sts, 2 dc in next 3 sts (20 sts)
RND 3: 1 dc in next 4 sts, (1 dc in next st, 2 dc in next st) 3 times, 1 dc in next 4 sts, (1 dc in next st, 2 dc in next st) 3 times .(26 sts)
RND 4: 1 dc in next 12 sts, pc in next st, 1 dc in next 6 sts, pc in next st, 1 dc in next 6 sts............................. (26 sts)
RND 5: 1 dc in next 12 sts, 1 dc in BLO leftover from pc in previous rnd, 1 dc in next 6 sts, 1 dc in BLO leftover from pc in previous rnd, 1 dc in next 6 sts .... (26 sts)
RND 6: 1 dc in each st..................... (26 sts)
Change to col 3.
RND 7: 1 dc in next 10 sts, then in FLO, 1 dc in next st, 2 dc in next st, 1 dc in next 2 sts, 2 dc in next st, 1 dc in next 3 sts, 2 dc in next st, 1 dc in next 2 sts, 2 dc in next st, 1 dc in next st, then in both loops, 1 dc in next 3 sts.......... (30 sts)
RND 8: 1 dc in next 8 sts, (2 dc in next st, 1 dc in next 3 sts) 5 times, 2 dc in next st .... (36 sts)
RND 9: 1 dc in each st..................... (36 sts)
RND 10: 1 dc in next 14 sts, (2 dc in next st, 1 dc in next 2 sts) 6 times, 1 dc in next 4 sts.............................. (42 sts)

RND 11: 1 dc in each st .... (42 sts)
RND 12: 1 dc in next 17 sts, (2 dc in next st, 1 dc in next 2 sts) 3 times, 1 dc in next st, (2 dc in next st, 1 dc in next 2 sts) 3 times, 1 dc in next 6 sts .... (48 sts)
RNDS 13-18: 1 dc in each st. (48 sts)
Insert safety eyes between rnds 9-10.
RND 19: (1 dc in next 6 sts, dc2tog) 6 times... (42 sts)
RND 20: (1 dc in next 5 sts, dc2tog) 6 times... (36 sts)
Start stuffing.
RND 21: (1 dc in next 4 sts, dc2tog) 6 times... (30 sts)
RND 22: (1 dc in next 3 sts, dc2tog) 6 times... (24 sts)
RND 23: (1 dc in next 2 sts, dc2tog) 6 times... (18 sts)
RND 24: (1 dc in next st, dc2tog) 6 times... (12 sts)
RND 25: dc2tog 6 times .... (6 sts)
Fasten off and close hole.

BODY

Using col 3, make magic ring.
RND 1: 6 dc in magic ring .... (6 sts)
RND 2: 2 dc in each st..................... (12 sts)
RND 3: (1 dc in next st, 2 dc in next st) 6 times... (18 sts)
RND 4: (1 dc in next 2 sts, 2 dc in next st) 6 times... (24 sts)
RND 5: (1 dc in next 3 sts, 2 dc in next st) 6 times... (30 sts)
RND 6: (1 dc in next 4 sts, 2 dc in next st) 6 times... (36 sts)
RND 7: (1 dc in next 8 sts, 2 dc in next st) 4 times... (40 sts)
RNDS 8-18: 1 dc in each st .... (40 sts)
RND 19: (1 dc in next 8 sts, dc2tog) 4 times... (36 sts)
RND 20: 1 dc in each st .... (36 sts)
RND 21: (1 dc in next 7 sts, dc2tog) 4 times... (32 sts)
Start stuffing.
RND 22: (1 dc in next 6 sts, dc2tog) 4 times... (28 sts)
RND 23: (1 dc in next 5 sts, dc2tog) 4 times... (24 sts)
RND 24: (1 dc in next 4 sts, dc2tog) 4 times... (20 sts)
RND 25: (1 dc in next 3 sts, dc2tog) 4 times... (16 sts)
Finish off, leaving long tail.
Sew last round of the body to the head between rnds 11-16, with the eyes at the top.

WIG

Using col 3, ch 7.
Start with a loop st and work the rest of this piece with alternating loop stitch and dc. For an inc stitch, make 1 loop st and 1 dc into same st.
RND 1: 1 dc in 3rd ch from hook, 1 dc into next 3 chs, 3 dc into the last ch, 1 dc into the back of each 4 chs, 3 dc into the space between the skipped chs 1 and 2 ... (14 sts)
RND 2: 1 dc in next 4 sts, 2 dc in next 3 sts, 1 dc in next 4 sts, 2 dc in next 3 sts ....(20 sts)
RND 3: 1 dc in next 4 sts, then (1 dc in next st, 2 dc in next st) 3 times, 1 dc in next 4 sts, then (1 dc in next st, 2 dc in next st) 3 times ....(26 sts)
RND 4: 1 dc in next 4 sts, then (1 dc in next 2 sts, 2 dc in next st) 3 times, 1 dc in next 4 sts, then (1 dc in next 2 sts, 2 dc in next st) 3 times ....(32 sts)
RND 5: 1 dc in next 4 sts, then (1 dc in next 3 sts, 2 dc in next st) 3 times, 1 dc in next 4 sts, then (1 dc in next 3 sts, 2 dc in next st) 3 times ....(38 sts)
Fasten off leaving long yarn tail.
Sew to the top middle of the head between RNDS 11-23.

HORNS

(Make 2)
Using col 2, make magic ring.
RND 1: 4 dc in magic ring ....(4 sts)
RND 2: (2 dc in next st, 1 dc in next st) 2 times..(6 sts)
RND 3: 1 dc in each st........................(6 sts)
RND 4: 2 dc in next st, 1 dc in next 5 sts (7 sts)
RND 5: 1 dc in next st, 2 dc in next st, 1 dc in next 5 sts..(8 sts)
RND 6: 1 dc in next 2 sts, 2 dc in next st, 1 dc in next 5 sts....................................(9 sts)
RND 7: 1 dc in next 3 sts, 2 dc in next st, 1 dc in next 5 sts.................................(10 sts)
RND 8: 1 dc in next 4 sts, 2 dc in next st, 1 dc in next 5 sts..................................(11 sts)
RND 9: 1 dc in each st.....................(11 sts)
Stuff firmly. Fasten off, leaving a long tail.
Sew to head between RNDS 14-18 on either side of the wig with the curved sides facing out.

EARS

(Make 2)
Using col 3, make magic ring.
RND 1: 4 dc in magic ring ....(4 sts)
RND 2: (2 dc in next st, 1 dc in next st) 2 times..(6 sts)

RND 3: (2 dc in next st, 1 dc in next 2 sts) 2 times..(8 sts)
RND 4: (2 dc in next st, 1 dc in next st) 4 times..(12 sts)
RND 5: (2 dc in next st, 1 dc in next 2 sts) 4 times..(16 sts)
RNDS 6-8: 1 dc in each st ....(16 sts)
RND 9: (1 dc in next 2 sts, dc2tog) 4 times..(12 sts)
RND 10: 1 dc in each st....................(12 sts)
Fasten off, leaving long tail.
Flatten piece and fold the bottom in half, sewing into shape. Sew to head between RNDS 14-18, below horns.

ARMS

(Make 2)
Using col 1, make magic ring.
RND 1: 6 dc in magic ring ....(6 sts)
RND 2: 2 dc in each st.....................(12 sts)
RND 3: (1 dc in next st, 2 dc in next st) 6 times..(18 sts)
RND 4: 1 dc in BLO of each st ....(18 sts)
RND 5: 1 dc in each st.....................(18 sts)
RND 6: (1 dc in next 7 sts, dc2tog) 2 times..(16 sts)
RND 7: (1 dc in next 2 sts, dc2tog) 4 times..(12 sts)
Change to col 3.
RNDS 8-17: 1 dc in each st... (12 sts)
Start stuffing.
RND 18: dc2tog 6 times ...... (6 sts)
Fasten off and close hole, leaving yarn tail to sew top of arm to body just below where the head is joined.

LEGS

(Make 2)
Using col 1, make magic ring.
RND 1: 6 dc in magic ring ....
(6 sts)
RND 2: 2 dc in each st............. (12 sts)
RND 3: (1 dc in next st, 2 dc in next st) 6 times..(18 sts)
RND 4: (1 dc in next 2 sts, 2 dc in next st) 6 times..(24 sts)
RND 5: 1 dc in BLO of each st .....(24 sts)
RND 6: 1 dc in each st..................(24 sts)
RND 7: 1 dc in next 6 sts, dc2tog, 1 dc in next st, dc2tog, 1 dc in next 2 sts, dc2tog, 1 dc in next st, dc2tog, 1 dc in next 6 sts..............
(20 sts)
RND 8: 1 dc in next 5 sts, dc2tog, 1 dc in next st, dc2tog 2 times, 1 dc in next st, dc2tog, 1 dc in

next 5 sts..
....(16 sts)
Change to col 3.
RNDS 9-18: 1 dc in each st.............. (16 sts)
RND 19: (1 dc in next 2 sts, dc2tog) 4 times..(12 sts)
RND 20: dc2tog 6 times ....(6 sts)
Fasten off, leaving long tail.
Sew legs to the side of the body, between RNDS 7-11.

TAIL

Using col 3, make magic ring.
RND 1: 4 dc in magic ring ....(4 sts)
RND 2: 2 dc in each st........................(8 sts)
RNDS 3-13: 1 dc in each st.................(8 sts)
Stuff lightly. Fasten off, leaving long tail.
Sew to back of the body, between RNDS 8-10.
Cut 8 strands of col 3 approx 6cm long. Fold a strand in half. Insert the hook between 2 sts of the first 2 rnds of the tail, hook the fold of the strand and pull through just until the loop appears. Pull loose ends of strand through loop, then pull snuggly the attach. Repeat with the other strands.

MAGICAL UNICORN

LEARN HOW TO EASILY BRING THIS MUCH-LOVED FANTASY
CREATURE INTO THE REAL WORLD – HORN AND ALL!

Pattern by:

Mevlinn Gusick

Mevlinn is a college graduate with a BFA in Fine Arts Painting. Her interest in knitting and crochet began when her aunt suggested she try knitting. It peaked her curiosity and here she is today, crocheting amigurumi whenever she gets the chance and giving them to those she loves.

www.mevvsan.com

You Will Need...

Yarn:
- 1 x 100g (295m) ball of aran weight yarn in:
- White.
- A small amount of Dark Pink
- Grey
- Yellow
- Light Pink

Tools:
- 2.75mm hook (US C/2)
- stitch marker

Other:
- Washable toy stuffing
- 9mm black safety eyes

Pattern

Finished product size: approx28 cm tall

★ **NOTE:** The body has a side specific decrease. This decrease is creating the 'rump' of the unicorn. Keep this in mind when you sew the head on later.

BODY

Using col 1, make a magic ring.
RND 1: 7 dc in magic ring............ (7 sts)
Place st marker in last st, and move this up at end of each round.
RND 2: 2 dc in each st around....(14 sts)
RND 3: (2 dc in next st, 1 dc in next st) 7 times....................................(21 sts)
RND 4: (2 dc in next st, 1 dc in next 2 sts) 7 times .... (28 sts)
RND 5: (2 dc in next st, 1 dc in next 3 sts) 7 times .... (35 sts)
RND 6: (2 dc in next st, 1 dc in next 4 sts) 7 times ....(42 sts)
RND 7: 1 dc in each st around....(42 sts)
RND 8: (2 dc in next st, dc in next 5 sts) 7 times.......................................(49 sts).
RND 9: 1 dc in each st around....(49 sts)
RNDS 10-12: dc2tog, 1 dc in each remaining st .... (46 sts after rnd 12)
RNDS 13-14: dc2tog, 1 dc in each st to the last 3 sts, dc2tog, 1 dc in last st........ ....(42 sts after rnd 14)
Stuff with fibrefill and continue stuffing as you go.
RNDS 15-22: dc2tog, 1 dc in each st to the last 3 sts, dc2tog, 1 dc in last st........ .... (26 sts after rnd 22)
RNDS 23-28: dc2tog, 1 dc in each remaining st .... (20 sts after rnd 28)
Fasten off leaving a tail for sewing. When the head is complete you will use this yarn end to sew the body and head together.

HEAD

Using col 1, make a magic ring.
RND 1: 6 dc in magic ring.............(6 sts)
RND 2: 2 dc in each st around .... (12 sts)
RND 3: (2 dc in next st, 1 dc in next st) 6 times..(18 sts)
RND 4: (2 dc in next st, 1 dc in next 2 sts) 6 times ....(24 sts)
RND 5: (2 dc in next st, 1 dc in next 3 sts) 6 times .... (30 sts)
RND 6: (2 dc in next st, 1 dc in next 4 sts) 6 times .... (36 sts)
RNDS 7-15: 1 dc in each st around. .... (36 sts)

Change to col 2.
RND 16: (2 dc in next st, 1 dc in next 5 sts) 6 times ....(42 sts)
Place eyes between rnds 12 and 13 with 10 sts between them.
RNDS 17-21: 1 dc in each st around........ (42 sts)
Stuff with fibrefill and continue stuffing as you go.
RND 22: (dc2tog, 1 dc in next 5 sts) 6 times........................ (36 sts)
RND 23: (dc2tog, 1 dc in next 4 sts) 6 times........................ (30 sts)
RND 24: (dc2tog, 1 dc in next 3 sts) 6 times..........................(24 sts)
RND 25: (dc2tog, 1 dc in next 2 sts) 6 times..........................(18 sts)
RND 26: (dc2tog, 1 dc in next st) 6 times..........................(12 sts)
RND 27: dc2tog 6 times ....(6 sts)
Fasten off, leaving a long tail for sewing.

Using your yarn needle, weave the yarn tail through the front ring of each remaining st and pull it tight to close. Sew head onto body. The back of the neck should sew onto rnd 6 of the head.

LEGS
(Make 2)
Using col 3, make a magic ring.
RND 1: 4 dc in magic ring.............(4 sts)
RND 2: 2 dc in each st around..... (8 sts)
RND 3: (2 dc in next st, 1 dc in next st) 4 times...(12 sts)
RND 4: 1 dc in each st around......(12 sts)
Change to col 1.
RNDS 5-17: 1 dc in each st around ....(12 sts)
Fasten off, leaving a tail for sewing. Lightly stuff the legs with more stuffing near the hooves.

ASSEMBLE THE LEGS
1 Start by sewing the back legs first. Place the horse on a flat surface in the seated position that you will want it to be, and pin the legs to the sides of the body.

2 Attach the back legs at rnds 6-8 of the body with 12 sts between the initial attachment points of each leg. Sew each leg about 8 sts down the leg against the body to stop them from bowing out.
   When the hind legs are attached, the unicorn should be able to sit well on its own, and this helps when sewing the front legs.

3 Attach the front legs at rnd 19 of the body with 4 sts between each leg. Sew each leg about 8 sts down the leg against the body to stop the front legs from bowing out.

EARS
(Make 2)
Using col 1, ch 5.
ROW 1: 1 dc in 2nd ch from hook, 1 dc in next 2 ch, 4 dc in last ch, rotate and work along the opposite side of the foundation ch, 1 dc in next 3 ch, turn(10 sts)
ROW 2: ch 1 (not counted as a st), 1 dc in next 3 sts, 2 dc in next 4 sts, 1 dc in next 3 sts, turn ....(14 sts)
ROW 3: ch 1 (not counted as a st), 1 dc in each st around ....(14 sts)

Fasten off, leaving a tail for sewing. Pinch the base of the ear together and sew the ears 6 rnds behind the eyes with 9 sts between each ear.

HORN
Using col 4, make a magic ring.
RND 1: 4 dc in magic ring.............(4 sts)
RNDS 2-6 (blo): 2 dc in next st, 1 dc in each remaining st......................................
.... (9 sts after rnd 6)
Fasten off, leaving a long tail for sewing. Sew the horn unstuffed onto the top of the head between the ears and the eyes.

TAIL
Cut 5 strands each of col 2 and col 5 that are 30cm in length.

1 Take one strand of each col and fold them in half. With the folded end between your fingers, insert your hook in the rump of your unicorn where you want the tail to be (about rnd 8 of the body), and place the folded ends of the yarn onto the hook and pull them back through the body.

2 Take the loose ends of the yarn, wrap them around the hook and pull them through the ring. Pull to tighten. Repeat this 4 more times in sts adjacent to the first st to create a thick tail.

3 Separate the strands into 3 sections and braid or plait them. Take a piece of col 4 and wrap it around the end of the braid, then tie it tightly with a bow.

MANE
Cut a few dozen strands each of cols 2 and 5 that are 25cm in length.

1 Find the centre of the unicorn's head and, using one strand at a time, attach the mane using the same method as given for the tail. To keep the mane straight, follow the sts down the back in a straight line until about 15 strands have been attached, alternating between col 2 and col 5.

2 Repeat to add another line on each side of the centre mane to create 3 lines in total. Trim and braid or plait the mane.

Tip
You could make a multicoloured rainbow mane and tail

OCTOPUS PLUSHIE

THIS TACTILE OCTOPUS TOY IS FUN FOR
LITTLE HANDS TO PLAY WITH

You Will Need...

Yarn:
- 1 x 100g (295m) ball of Stylecraft Special DK in:
- Pink Blush (1833)
- A small amount of Black (1002)*

Tools:
- 3.5mm hook (US E/4)
- Stitch marker

Other:
- Fibrefill stuffing
- Washable toy stuffing

Pattern

Finished product size: Approx20cm/8in long (with tentacles laid out flat).
- ★ **TENSION:** 20 stitches and 21 rounds, to 10 x 10cm, over double crochet, using 3.5mm hook.
- ★ **NOTE:** Body is made in rounds that are worked in a continuous spiral. Place stitch marker at the end of each round and move this up as you work.
- ★ When working in rounds, the right side is on the outside. Yarn amounts are based on average requirements and are therefore approximate. Instructions in square brackets are worked as stated after 2nd bracket.

BODY

Starting at top.
With 3.5mm hook and Pink, ch 2.
RND 1: 6 dc in 2nd ch from hook. (6 sts)
Place st marker in last st, and move this up at end of each round.
RND 2: 2 dc in each st .... (12 sts)
RND 3: (2 dc in next st, 1 dc in next st) to end........................... (18 sts)
RND 4: (2 dc in next st, 1 dc in next 2 sts) to end .... (24 sts)
RND 5: (2 dc in next st, 1 dc in next 3 sts) to end .... (30 sts)
RND 6: (2 dc in next st, 1 dc in next 4 sts) to end .... (36 sts)
RND 7: (2 dc in next st, 1 dc in next 5 sts) to end .... (42 sts)
RNDS 8-19: 1 dc in each st .... (42 sts)

RND 20: (dc2tog, 1 dc in next 5 sts) to end ....(36 sts)
RND 21: 1 dc in each st ....(36 sts)
RND 22: (dc2tog, 1 dc in next 4 sts) to end ....(30 sts)
RND 23: (dc2tog, 1 dc in next 3 sts) to end ....(24 sts)
RND 24: (dc2tog, 1 dc in next 2 sts) to end. ....(18 sts)
RND 25: (dc2tog, 1 dc in next st) to end (12 sts)
Stuff body.
RND 26: dc2tog to end ....(6 sts)
Fasten off. Add more stuffing if required then close gap in body.

TENTACLES

With 3.5mm hook and Pink, ch 70.

ROW 1: 1 dc in 2nd ch from hook, 1 dc in each ch ....(69 sts)
ROW 2: ch 1 (does not count as a st), (dc2tog, 1 dc in next st) to end........ (46 sts)
ROW 3: ch 1 (does not count as a st), (dc2tog, 1 dc in next st) to last st, 1 dc in last st ....(31 sts)
Fasten off.

TO MAKE UP

Pin one end of each tentacle to underside of body so they are evenly spaced. Sew in place. With Black, embroider a few vertical stitches for the eyes and sew a small 'V' for the mouth to make a cute expression.

DOLLS & BEARS

MEXICAN DOLL AMIGURUMI

A VIBRANT DOLL THAT WILL BE RIGHT AT HOME IN A COLOURFUL TOYBOX

Every child loves a splash of colour, and that's one of the reasons why this doll is perfect for kids of all ages. To be on the safe side, though, use black thread or yarn to embroider the eyes if you're giving this toy to a toddler or baby.

Why not mix up the colours, too? They could be your child's favourite colours, or they could match the nursery. The possibilities are endless!

Pattern by:

Anitha Arputha Sundary

Hello! I'm Anitha, an amigurumi designer and crochet blogger from India. I like to design cute and quirky amigurumis that are easier to make for beginners. You can find lots of beginner friendly free amigurumi patterns on my blog.

www.littleloveeveryday.com

You Will Need...

Yarn:
- You will need to use 4 ply (sport) weight yarn in your chosen colours. Here we have used:
- Colour 1: Cream
- Colour 2: White
- Colour 3: Black
- Colour 4: Blue
- Colour 5: Lavender
- Colour 6: Green
- Colour 7: Red
- Colour 8: Yellow

Tools:
- 2.5mm hook (US B/1 or C/2)
- Yarn needle
- Stitch marker
- Scissors

Other:
- Fibrefill stuffing
- A pair of 6mm safety eyes
- Black embroidery thread
- Sewing pins

Pattern

* **NOTE:** This pattern is worked in continuous rounds unless stated otherwise. Use a stitch marker at the end of each round.

HEAD
With col 1, make a magic ring.
RND 1: 6 dc in magic ring..............(6 sts)
RND 2: 2 dc in each st ....(12 sts)
RND 3: (1 dc in next st, 2 dc in next st) 6 times..............................(18 sts)
RND 4: (1 dc in next 2 sts, 2 dc in next st) 6 times.....................(24 sts)
RND 5: (1 dc in next 3 sts, 2 dc in next st) 6 times.....................(30 sts)
RND 6: (1 dc in next 4 sts, 2 dc in next st) 6 times.....................(36 sts)
RNDS 7-11: 1 dc in each st...........(36 sts)

RND 12: (1 dc in next 4 sts, dc2tog) 6 times............................(30 sts)
RND 13: (1 dc in next 3 sts, dc2tog) 6 times............................(24 sts)
Attach 6mm safety eyes between rnds 10 and 11, 6 stitches apart.
RND 14: (1 dc in next 2 sts, dc2tog) 6 times............................(18 sts)
RND 15: (1 dc in next st, dc2tog) 6 times (12 sts)
Stuff the head firmly with fiberfill.
Fasten off leaving a long tail for sewing.

Tip

If you don't want to use safety eyes, you can embroider the eyes with black thread.

HANDS

(Make 2)

With col 1, make magic ring.

RND 1: 6 dc in magic ring.............(6 sts)

RNDS 2-4: 1 dc in each st.............(6 sts)

Switch to col 2.

RND 5: 1 dc in each st ....(6 sts)

RND 6: 1 dc through both the layers of the arms to close..........................(3 sts)

Fasten off, leaving a long tail for sewing.

LEGS

(Make 2)

With col 2, make magic ring.

RND 1: 6 dc in magic ring.............(6 sts)

RND 2: (1 dc in next 2 sts, 2 dc in next st) 2 times......................................(8 sts)

RNDS 3-11: 1 dc in each st ....(8 sts)

Fasten off the first leg but don't cut the yarn in second leg. Stuff the legs.

BODY

(continued from the legs)

RND 12: With the 2nd leg, ch 2, join to the 1st leg and dc around, dc in the 2 chs, dc around the second leg and dc in the other side of 2 chs ....(20 sts)

RND 13: 1 dc in each st ....(20 sts)

RND 14: (1 dc in next 8 sts, dc2tog) 2 times................................(18 sts)

RND 15: 1 dc in BLO of each st ....
....(18 sts)

RND 16: (1 dc in next 4 sts, dc2tog) 3 times................................(15 sts)

RND 17: 1 dc in each st...............(15 sts)

RND 18: (1 dc in next 3 sts, dc2tog) 3 times................................(12 sts)

RND 19: 1 dc in each st ....(12 sts)

Stuff body. Fasten off and sew ends.

SKIRT

Note: ch 1 at the start of each row and sl st to first htr when you reach at the end of each row.

Join col 3 to the front loops at rnd 15 of the body.

ROW 1: (1 htr in next 2 sts, 2 htr in next st) 6 times....................................(24 sts)

ROW 2: 1 htr in each st...............(24 sts)

ROW 3: In BLO, (1 htr in next 3 sts, 2 htr in next st) 6 times ....(30 sts)

ROW 4: 1 htr in each st...............(30 sts)

ROW 5: In BLO (1 htr in next 4 sts, 2 htr in next st) 6 times ....(36 sts)

ROW 6: 1 htr in each st...............(36 sts)

ROW 7: In BLO, (1 htr in next 5 sts, 2 htr in next st) 6 times ....(42 sts)

ROW 8: 1 htr in each st...............(42 sts)

ROW 9: In BLO, 1 dc in each st ...(42 sts)

Fasten off and sew the ends.

Crocheting the coloured bands on the skirt

SKIRT FRILLS

Begin with ch 1 at the start of each row and sl st at the end of each row.

Join col 8 to the front loops of row 3 of the skirt and work 1 dc in each st. Fasten off.

Join col 6 to the front loops of row 5 of the skirt and work 1 dc in each st. Fasten off.

Join col 4 to the front loops of row 7 of the skirt and work 1 dc in each st. Fasten off.

Join col 5 to the front loops of row 9 of the skirt and work 1 dc in each st. Fasten off. Sew in all ends.

WAIST BELT

With col 7, ch 20 and sl st to the first stitch to form a ring.

RND 1: Ch 1, sl st in each st.........(20 sts)
Fasten off leaving a long tail for sewing.

HAIR

With col 3, make magic ring.
RND 1: 6 dc in magic ring..............(6 sts)

RND 2: 2 dc in each st ....(12 sts)
RND 3: (1 dc in next st, 2 dc in next st) 6 times..(18 sts)
RND 4: (1 dc in next 2 sts, 2 dc in next st) 6 times....................................(24 sts)
RND 5: (1 dc in next 3 sts, 2 dc in next st) 6 times....................................(30 sts)
RND 6: (1 dc in next 4 sts, 2 dc in next st) 6 times....................................(36 sts)
RNDS 7-9: 1 dc in each st. (36 sts)
RNDS 10-11 are working in rows instead of continuous rounds.
ROW 10 and RND 12 are only worked as half a round, rather than complete rounds.
ROW 10: 1 dc in next 3 sts, 1 htr in next 16 sts, 1 dc in next st, sl st, ch 1, turn.
ROW 11: Skip the sl st space of row 10 and 1 dc, 16 htr, 3 dc (place the stitch marker here and continue) 1 dc in next 3 sts, 1 htr in next 11 sts, 1 dc in next st, sl st, ch 1, turn.
RND 12: Skip the sl st space of the previous row. 1 dc in next st, 1 htr in next 11 sts, 1 dc in next 3 sts. Do not

turn.
RND 13: Place stitch marker at the end of rnd 12. 1 dc in next 20 sts, sl st in previous sl st space, 1 dc in next 15 sts. Fasten off leaving a long tail for sewing.

HEADBAND

With col 3, ch 38 and sl st to the first st to form a ring.

RND 1: ch 2, 1 dc in each st, sl st to the first dc ....(38 sts)
Fasten off leaving a long tail for sewing.

RIBBONS

Using any yarn colour of your choice, ch 7 and sl st to the first chain to form a ring.

RND 1: Ch 2, 1 htr in each st, sl st to the first st..(7 sts)
Fasten off leaving a long tail for sewing. Make around 13 ribbons in different colours.

EARRINGS

(Make 2)

With col 4, work 4 dc in a magic ring. Fasten off leaving a long tail for sewing.

ASSEMBLY

1 Sew the hair to the head.

2 Place the head band so that it aligns with rnd 11 of hair at the front and sew.

3 Place the ribbons over the head band and stitch them. Use sewing pins to keep the ribbons in place.

4 Sew the earrings below the hairline at the side of the head.

5 Embroider the mouth using black embroidery thread.

6 Insert the waist belt through the top of the body and sew it just above the skirt.

7 Attach the head to the body.

8 Embroider a half square shape using lavender colour yarn for the blouse design.

9 Finally attach the arms on body just below the head.

LITTLE DRESS-UP DOLL

Pattern by:

Amy Kember

Amy is a technical writer living in Ottawa, Canada. Her interest in crochet began when she discovered an amigurumi book in a used bookstore. After making a pig, she was instantly hooked. Since 2010, Amy has been designing and selling her own amigurumi patterns on Etsy.

www.etsy.com/shop/
AmysGurumis

You Will Need...

Yarn:
- You will need to use worsted weight yarn in your chosen colours. Here we have used Bernat Handicrafter Cotton in:
- Colour 1: Parchment (2 balls)
- Colour 2: Warm Brown (1 ball)
- Colour 3: French Blue (1 ball)
- Colour 4: Country Red (oddment)
- Colour 5: Black (oddment)

Tools:
- 3.25mm hook (US D/3)
- Yarn needle

Other:
- Fibrefill stuffing
- 1 pair 6 mm safety eyes

LITTLE DRESS-UP DOLL'S HEAD, BODY AND LEGS ARE CROCHETED AS ONE PIECE SO THERE ARE FEWER PIECES TO ASSEMBLE

Pattern

Finished product size: approx 22cm/8.6in tall

* **NOTE:** Each piece is worked in a continuous spiral unless stated otherwise.

HEAD, BODY AND LEGS

Using 3.25mm hook and col 1, make a magic ring.

RND 1: 6 dc into the ring and pull it closed... (6 sts)
RND 2: 2 dc in each st. .... (12 sts)
RND 3: (1 dc in next st, 2 dc in next st) 6 times...(18 sts)
RND 4: (1 dc in next 2 sts, 2 dc in next st) 6 times................................... (24 sts)
RND 5: (1 dc in next 3 sts, 2 dc in next st) 6 times................................... (30 sts)
RNDS 6-13: 1 dc in each st. ....(30 sts)
RND 14: (1 dc in next 3 sts, dc2tog) 6 times...(24 sts)
RND 15: (1 dc in next 2 sts, dc2tog) 6 times...(18 sts)

ASSEMBLE THE FACE

Insert 6mm safety eyes between RNDS 9 and 10 of the head and position them 3 stitches apart.

Embroider a mouth between the eyes on RNDS 12 and 13 using a yarn needle and black yarn. Stuff the head firmly.

RND 16: (1 dc in next st, dc2tog) 6 times...(12 sts)
RND 17: dc2tog 6 times ....(6 sts)
RND 18: 2 dc in each st .... (12 sts)
RND 19: (1 dc in next st, 2 dc in next st)

6 times. ....(18 sts)
RND 20: (1 dc in next 2 sts, 2 dc in next st) 6 times................................... (24 sts)
RND 21-32: 1 dc in each st. .... (24 sts)
Stuff the body firmly.

MAKE LEGS

Insert hook in the 12th dc of RND 32 and join with ss to separate body into 2 sections for the legs (adjust the dc that you insert the hook into to make sure that the space where the body divides lines up with the eyes and mouth in the middle of the head).

RNDS 33-46: 1 dc in each st around the 1st half of the body to form the 1st leg . (12 sts)
Fasten off.
Insert crochet hook into a dc on the 2nd leg opening.
RNDS 1-14: 1 dc in each st around the 2nd half of the body to form the 2nd leg (12 sts)
Stuff the legs firmly.

EARS
(Make 2)
Using col 1, make a magic ring.
Work 6 dc into ring and pull it closed. Fasten off.

ARMS
(Make 2)
Using col 1, make a magic ring.
RND 1: 4 dc into ring and pull it closed. (4 sts)
RND 2: 2 dc in each st. .... (8 sts)
RNDS 3-5: 1 dc in each st..............(8 sts)
RND 6: dc2tog 4 times .... (4 sts)
RND 7: 2 dc in each st .... (8 sts)
RNDS 8-19: 1 dc in each dc ....(8 sts)
Fasten off.

FEET
(Make 2)
Using col 1, make a magic ring.
RND 1: 6 dc into ring and pull it closed (6 sts)
RND 2: 2 dc in each st ....(12 sts)
RND 3: (2 dc in next 3 sts, 1 dc in next 3 sts) 2 times .... (18 sts)
RND 4: 1 tr in next 10 sts, 1 dc in next 8 sts. .... (18 sts)
RND 5: dc2tog 5 times, 1 dc in next 8 sts .... (13 sts)
Fasten off.

HAIR
(Make 2)
Using col 2, make a magic ring.
RND 1: 6 dc into ring and pull it closed. (6 sts)
RND 2: 2 dc in each st .... (12 sts)
RND 3: (1 dc in next st, 2 dc in next st) 6 times ....(18 sts)
RND 4: (1 dc in next 2 sts, 2 dc in next st) 6 times.................................. (24 sts)
Now we switch from rounds to rows.
RND 5 (1 dc in next 3 sts, 2 dc in next st) 6 times, turn .... (30 sts)
ROW 6: ch 1, 1 dc in next 10 sts, 1 tr in next 10 sts, turn ....

.... (20 sts, leaving 10 sts unworked)
ROW 7: ch 1, 1 tr in next 10 sts, 1 dc in next 10 sts, turn .... (20 sts)
ROW 8: ch 1, 1 dc in next 10 sts, 1 tr in next st, turn .... (20 sts)
ROWS 9-11: ch 1, 1 dc in each st, turn. . (3 rows of 20 sts)

FORM CURLS
ROW 12 (FORM CURLS): *ch 16, begin with 2nd ch from hook, 1 ss in each of next 15 ch, skip 1 dc, ss in next dc (one curl formed); repeat from * to last st, ch 16, begin with 2nd ch from hook, 1 ss in each of next 15 ch, ss in next dc(10 curls made)
Fasten off leaving a long tail.

DRESS
Using col 3, ch 21.
ROW 1: 1 dc into 2nd ch from hook, 1 dc in each ch to end, turn........... (20 sts)
ROW 2: ch 1, (1 dc in next 3 sts, 2 dc in next st) 4 times, 1 dc in next 4 sts, turn . (24 sts)
ROW 3: ch 1, (1 dc in next 4 sts, 2 dc in next st) 4 times, 1 dc in next 4 sts, turn . (28 sts)
ROW 4: ch 1, (1 dc in next 5 sts, 2 dc in next st) 4 times, 1 dc in next 4 sts, turn . (32 sts)
ROW 5: ch 1, (1 dc in next 6 sts, 2 dc in next st) 4 times, 1 dc in next 4 sts, turn . (36 sts)
ROW 6: ch 1, 1 dc in each st, turn .... (36 sts)

MAKE SLEEVES
Now we switch from rows to rounds.
RND 7: ch 1, 1 dc in next 5 sts, ch 2, skip 7 sts, join in 13th st with ss, 1 dc in next 10 sts, ch 2, skip 7 sts, join in 31st st with ss, 1 dc in next 5 sts, join with ss and begin working in rnds...................... .... (24 sts)

NOTE: Do not count the slip sts from this rnd as sts in the following rnd)

RNDS 8-11: 1 dc in each st. ....(24 sts)
RND 12: (1 tr in next st, 2 tr in next st) 12 times......................................(36 sts)
RNDS 13-15: 1 tr in each st.........(36 sts)
RND 16: 1 tr in each st to last 3 sts, 1 htr, 1 dc, ss into last dc. (avoids jog at join.)
Fasten off.

ASSEMBLE THE DRESS
To finish off the dress, ch 3 and ss into the 1st st at the top of the dress (to form the button hole), then continue to ss along the opening of the dress until you reach the opposite side of the opening and fasten off.

Using the other yarn end on the left side of the dress opening and a yarn needle, fasten a white button to the dress and weave in the ends.

SHOES
(Make 2)
Using col 4, make a magic ring.
RND 1: 6 dc into ring and pull it closed . (6 sts)
RND 2: 2 dc in each st .... (12 sts)
RND 3: (2 dc in next 3 sts, 1 dc in next 3 sts) twice. ....(18 sts)
RND 4: 1 tr in next 10 sts, 1 dc in next 8 sts .... (18 sts)
RND 5: dc2tog 5 times, 1 dc in next 8 sts, do not fasten off................... (13 sts)

MAKE SHOE STRAP
Ch 5, skip 4 dc, join in 5th dc with ss. Fasten off.

FINISHING
1 Stuff the arms and feet.

2 Sew the hair to the head (stitch up the side of the head, along the front, down the other side of the head and then in between the hair piece and the curls along the back).

3 Sew the ears to the head.

4 Sew the arms to the body between rnd 19 and rnd 20 and position them 8 stitches apart in the front

5 Sew the feet to the bottom of the legs.

Pattern by:

Jennifer Percival

Jennifer creates amigurumi with kids (and kids at heart) in mind. She enjoys designs that encourage imagination and feature classic stories and holidays.

@crochettoplay
www.CrochetToPlay.com

You Will Need...

Yarn:
- You will need to use aran weight yarn in your chosen colours. Here we have used Paintbox Cotton Aran in:
- Colour 1: Soft Fudge (2 balls)
- Colour 3: Spearmint Green (1 ball)
- Colour 4: Pure Black (1 ball)
- We have also used Yarn and Colors Epic in:
- Colour 2: Bronze (1 ball) measurements

Tools:
- 3.5mm hook (US E/4)
- Stitch marker
- Yarn needle

Other:
- Fibrefill stuffing
- Two 9mm safety eyes
- Four 20mm plastic doll joints

THE PUMPKIN PATCH BEAR

PERFECT FOR AUTUMN, THIS LITTLE GUY WILL BRING A SMILE TO EVERYONE'S FACE

Pattern

Finished product size: 19cm/7½in tall when sitting, 25cm/10in when legs are outstretched

* **NOTES:** Most pieces are worked in a spiral, without joining each round. It may help to use a stitch marker to mark the first stitch of the round, and move it up as you work each round.

*Some pieces start with a magic ring, worked as follows: wind yarn around the index finger of your left hand to form a ring, insert hook into ring, yoh and pull a loop through, ch 1, (does not count as a st), work rnd 1 into the ring, then pull end of yarn tightly to close the hole. Make sure that when you crochet into the ring, that you crochet over the twisted strands of yarn that sit to the left of your hook. Alternatively, you could make 2 ch then work rnd 1 into the 2nd chain from hook

* **SPECIAL STITCHES:** Insert your hook through the front loop of the indicated st, then insert your hook into the front loop of the next st. Your hook is now inserted into the front loops of both stitches you'd like to decrease into one stitch, yoh and draw up loop through both sts, then yoh and pull through two loops on hook.

EARS
(Make 2)
Using col 1, make a magic ring.
RND 1: 6 dc into magic ring .... (6 sts)
RND 2: 2 dc in each st around, turn .... (12 sts)
RND 3: 1 dc in each st .... (12 sts)
Fasten off, leaving long tail for attaching. Set aside.

SNOUT
RNDS 1-2: Using col 1, repeat rnds 1-2 of ears..(12 sts)
RND 3: (2 dc in next 3 sts, 1 dc in next 3 sts) twice .... (18 sts)
RNDS 4-5: 1 dc in each st...................... .... (18 sts)
Fasten off, leaving a long tail for attaching.
Using col 4 and yarn needle, embroider a nose in the shape of a triangle with a line coming straight down. Set aside.

HEAD
Using col 1, make a magic ring.
RND 1 (RS): 6 dc in a magic ring .... (6 sts)
RND 2: 2 dc in each st .... (12 sts)
RND 3: (1 dc in next st, 2 dc in next st) 6 times... (18 sts)
RND 4: (1 dc in next 2 sts, 2 dc in next st) 6 times................................. (24 sts)
RND 5: (1 dc in next 3 sts, 2 dc in next st) 6 times.................................(30 sts)
RND 6: (1 dc in next 4 sts, 2 dc in next st) 6 times................................(36 sts)
RND 7: (1 dc in next 5 sts, 2 dc in next st) 6 times ....(42 sts)
RND 8: (1 dc in next 6 sts, 2 dc in next st) 6 times................................. (48 sts)
RNDS 9-13: 1 dc in each st......(48 sts)
RND 14: (1 dc in next 7 sts, 2 dc in next st) 6 times.................................. (54 sts)
RNDS 15-16: 1 dc in each st ....(54 sts)
RND 17: (1 dc in next 7 sts, dc2tog) 6 times..(48 sts)

RND 18: (1 dc in next 6 sts, dc2tog) 6 times..(42 sts)
RND 19: (1 dc in next 5 sts, dc2tog) 6 times.......................................(36 sts)
RND 20: (1 dc in next 4 sts, dc2tog) 6 times.......................................(30 sts)
RND 21: (1 dc in next 3 sts, dc2tog) 6 times.......................................(24 sts)
RND 22: (1 dc in next 2 sts, dc2tog) 6 times..(18 sts)
Attach snout onto the lower third of the head, adding a little stuffing underneath. Attach safety eyes between rnds 12 and 13, about 12 sts apart. Attach the ears so that the top edge of the ear is at rnd 5, with ears 8-9 sts apart (across top of head).

Alternatively, you can wait to attach the ears until adding the hat to make sure they are perfectly lined up.
Stuff the head.
RND 23: (1 dc in next st, dc2tog) 6 times..(12 sts)
RND 24: dc2tog until closed.
Fasten off, using yarn needle to pull tightly through final stitches to close completely. Weave in end.

PUMPKIN BODY

RNDS 1-6: Using col 2, rep rnds 1-6 of head ....(36 sts)
RND 7: (1 dc in next 4 sts, 2 htr in next 2 sts) 6 times ....(48 sts)
RND 8: (1 dc in next 4 sts, 2 htr in next 4 sts) 6 times ....(72 sts)
RND 9: (dc2tog, 1 dc in next 10 sts) 6 times...(66 sts)
RND 10: (dc2tog, 1 dc in next 9 sts) 6 times...(60 sts)
RNDS 11-16: 1 dc in each st.........(60 sts)
RND 17: (dc2tog, 1 dc in next 8 sts) 6 times.......................................(54 sts)
RND 18: (dc2tog, 1 dc in next 7 sts) 6 times.......................................(48 sts)
RND 19: 1 dc in each st ....(48 sts)
RND 20: (dc2tog, 1 dc in next 6 sts) 6 times.......................................(42 sts)
RND 21: 1 dc in each st ....(42 sts)
RND 22: (dc2tog, 1 dc in next 5 sts) 6 times.......................................(36 sts)
RND 23: (dc2tog, 1 dc in next 4 sts) 6 times.......................................(30 sts)
RND 24: (dc2tog, 1 dc in next 3 sts) 6 times.......................................(24 sts)
RND 25: (dc2tog, 1 dc in next 2 sts) 6 times.......................................(18 sts)

Fasten off, leaving a very long tail (wrap loosely six times before trimming). If you turn your pumpkin body upside-down, you'll see that there are six curves and six indentations around its base. Use your yarn needle to bring yarn under a stitch from rnd 25 over the first indentation, then tack down by weaving under the initial magic ring at pumpkin base. Bring yarn back up and over the indentation on the opposite side. Repeat twice more, spacing grooves evenly every 3 sts of rnd 25. Leave unstuffed for now.

ARMS
(Make 2)
Stuff lightly as you go
RNDS 1-3: using col 1, rep rnds 1-3 of head ....(18 sts)
RND 4: 1 dc in each st .... (18 sts)
RND 5: (1 dc in next 4 sts, dc2tog) 3 times..(15 sts)
RND 6: 1 dc in each st .... (15 sts)
RND 7: (1 dc in next 3 sts, invdec) 3 times...(12 sts)
RNDS 8-16: 1 dc in each st .... (12 sts)
Insert plastic joint between rnd 14 and

15, and finish stuffing to desired fullness.

RND 17: (1 dc in next st, dc2tog) 4 times.. (8 sts)
Use yarn needle to pull through final stitches tightly into a ring, then fasten off securely.

Insert arm joints into opposite sides of body, lined up with 'grooves', about three rows down from the top round of the pumpkin body. Secure arm joints from the inside

LEGS
(Make 2)
Stuff lightly as you go.
RNDS 1-3: using col 1, rep rnds 1-3 of head ....(18 sts)
RND 4: (2 dc in next 3 sts, 1 dc in next 6 sts) 2 times ....(24 sts)
RND 5: 1 dc in each st ....(24 sts)
RND 6: (1 dc in next 2 sts, dc2tog) 6 times..(18 sts)
RND 7: 1 dc in next 6 sts, then dc2tog 3 times, 1 dc in last 6 sts.................(15 sts)
RNDS 8-18: 1 dc in each st .... (15 sts)
RND 19: (1 dc in next 3 sts, dc2tog) 3 times...(12 sts)
RND 20: 1 dc in each st ....(12 sts)
Insert plastic joint between rnds 18 and 19, and finish stuffing to desired fullness. Make sure the stems of the joints face towards the body.
RND 21: (1 dc in next st, dc2tog) 4 times...(8 sts)
Use yarn needle to pull through final stitches tightly into a ring, then fasten off securely. Insert leg joints into opposite sides of the body, directly below arms, about 15 rows down from the top round of the pumpkin body. Secure leg joints from the inside.

Stuff pumpkin body and use yarn needle and col 1 to attach head.

PUMPKIN HAT
The hat begins with the stem.
Using col 3, make a magic ring.
RND 1: 5 dc in magic ring............ (5 sts)
RNDS 2-4: 1 dc in each st.............(5 sts)
RND 5: using col 2, 2 dc in each st around. ....(10 sts)
RND 6: (1 dc in next st, 2 dc in next st) 5 times...(15 sts)
RND 7: (1 dc in next 4 sts, 2 dc in next st) 3 times....................................(18 sts)

RND 8: (1 dc in next 2 sts, 2 dc in next st) 6 times....................................(24 sts)
RND 9: (1 dc in next 3 sts, 2 dc in next st) 6 times................................... (30 sts)
RND 10: 1 dc in next 9 sts, ch 8 (for ear), skip 2 sts, 1 dc in next 8 sts, ch 8 (for ear), skip 2 sts, 1 dc in last 9 sts. .... (42 sts)
RND 11: 1 dc in each st, including ch sts . (42 sts)
RND 12: (1 dc in next 6 sts, 2 dc in next st) 6 times..........................(48 sts)
RND 13: 1 dc in each st ....(48 sts)

VINE
Ch 8, 2 dc in 2nd ch from hook and in each ch to end ....(14 sts)
Twist into a spiral as you go. Attach near stem on hat.

Weave in all ends. Place hat on bear's head with ears poking through.

TOYS

Pattern by:

Tanya Eberhardt

I am the heart and hands behind Little Things Blogged. I spent most of the time crocheting or knitting new things and share them on my blog and on Instagram.

www.littlethingsblogged.com

You Will Need...

Yarn:
- Small amounts of DK yarn in various colours

Tools:
- 3mm crochet hook
- Yarn needle
- Stitch marker

Other:
- Fibrefill stuffing
- Pom poms for decoration

CROCHET CAKE

A SWEET TREAT FOR THE KIDS WHO LOVE CONFECTIONS

If you're making toys for a child who loves their sweet treats, this cake is perfect. The pom pom decorations add an extra flair, but you could also crochet your own candles.

For more delicious creations, head to page 102 to find out how to make a burger, soda, ketchup bottle, hot dog and peanut butter and jelly on toast. Just make sure you have something to eat first, or you might find your tummy rumbling…

Pattern

* **NOTE:** To change colors, crochet to the last stitch on the row. Start the last stitch by inserting the hook into the chain from the previous row and pulling a loop through. Now, with the new color, finish the stitch by bringing a loop through the 2 loops on the hook.

The cake is crocheted in five pieces and then sewed together.

CAKE SIDES

(Make 2)

With white, ch 16.
ROW 1: 1 dc in 2nd ch from hook, 1 dc in next 14 chs, ch 1, turn........................ (15 sts)
ROWS 2-3: 1 dc in each st, ch 1, turn...........
....(15 sts)
Change to brown.
ROW 4: 1 dc in each st, ch 1, turn..... (15 sts)
Change to pink.
ROWS 5-8: 1 dc in each st, ch 1, turn ....
....(15 sts)
Change to brown.
ROW 9: 1 dc in each st, ch 1, turn..... (15 sts)
Change to white.
ROWS 10-12: 1 dc in each st, ch 1, turn ......
....(15 sts)
Change to pink.
ROW 13: 1 dc in each st, ch 1, turn ....

....(15 sts)
Finish off, leaving a long tail for sewing.

BACK

With pink, ch 15.
ROW 1: 1 dc in 2nd ch from hook, 1 dc in next 13 chs, ch 1, turn......................... (14 sts)
ROWS 2-13: 1 dc in each st, ch 1, turn .... (14 sts)
Finish off, leaving a long tail for sewing.

BOTTOM / TOP

(Make 1 each)

The bottom and the top are made using the same pattern. One needs to be pink and the other white.
With pink or white, ch 15.
ROW 1: 1 dc in 2nd ch from hook, 1 dc in next 13 chs, ch 1, turn......................... (14 sts)
ROW 2: dc2tog, 1 dc in next 10 sts, dc2tog, ch 1, turn............................... (12 sts)

Tip

Why not add some velcro to the sides so you can cut slices off like the real thing?

ROW 3: 1 dc in each st, ch 1, turn..... (12 sts)
ROW 4: dc2tog, 1 dc in next 8 sts, dc2tog, ch 1, turn .... (10 sts)
ROW 5: 1 dc in each st, ch 1, turn..... (10 sts)
ROW 6: dc2tog, 1 dc in next 6 sts, dc2tog, ch 1, turn .... (8 sts)
ROW 7: 1 dc in each st, ch 1, turn....... (8 sts)
ROW 8: dc2tog, 1 dc in next 4 sts, dc2tog, ch 1, turn .... (6 sts)
ROW 9: 1 dc in each st, ch 1, turn....... (6 sts)
ROW 10: dc2tog, 1 dc in next 2 sts, dc2tog, ch 1, turn.................................. (4 sts)
ROW 11: 1 dc in each st, ch 1, turn..... (4 sts)
ROW 12: dc2tog twice, ch 1, turn ...... (2 sts)
ROW 13: 1 dc in each st, ch 1, turn .... (2 sts)
ROW 14: dc2tog, ch 1, turn...................(1 st)
ROW 15: 1 dc..(1 st)
Finish off and leave a long tail for sewing.

ASSEMBLY

Sew the two sides to the back using a yarn needle. Sew the bottom and fill with fibrefill. Sew the top, continue to stuff and finish off. Add some pom poms as decoration.

Pattern by:

Erin Sharp

Erin is an avid crocheter and crafter with a love for yarn, creativity, and baked goods. She's been running her blog, The Cookie Snob, since 2015. Her biggest inspirations are her three children and their growing imaginations.

www.cookiesnobcrochet.com

You Will Need...

Yarn:

- You will need to use cotton Aran weight yarn in your chosen colours. Here we have used I Loved This Cotton! yarn in:
- Colour 1: White (10 yds)
- Colour 2: Pewter (105 yds)
- Colour 3: Dove (15 yds)
- Colour 4: Black (10 yds)
- Colour 5: Turquoise (55 yds)

Tools:

- 3.75mm crochet hook
- Yarn needle
- Stitch markers

Other:

- A pair of 10mm safety eyes
- Fibrefill stuffing

LENS

This section is worked in separate rounds. At the end of each round, sl st to first st to join.
Using col 1, make a magic ring.
RND 1: 6 dc in magic ring, ss to join, and pull taut to close the circle .... (6 sts)
RND 2: ch 1, 2 dc in each st .... (12 sts)
RND 3: ch 1, (2 dc in next st, 1 dc in next st) 6 times .... (18 sts)

CUDDLY CAMERA PLUSHIE

THE PERFECT ACCESSORY FOR SMALL BUDDING PHOTOGRAPHERS

Everyone's taking pictures these days, whether it's selfies or photos of the family you can look at for years to come. Now the youngest ones can get in on the fun with this adorable plushie.

While the kids enjoy snapping away, you don't have to worry about them dropping an expensive camera or phone. In fact, this toy is so soft and squishy, they might just want to cuddle with it instead!

Pattern

Finished product size: approx 14cm/5.5in wide and 10cm/4in tall, excluding the strap
★ **GAUGE:** 2in = 9 dc sts, 2in = 10 rows of dc sts

RND 4: ch 1, (1 dc in next st, 2 dc in next st, 1 dc in next st) 6 times .... (24 sts)
RND 5: ch 1, (2 dc in next st, 1 dc in next 3 sts) 6 times .... (30 sts)
Change to col 2.
RND 6: ch 1, in FLO (1 dc in next 2 sts, 2 dc in next st, 1 dc in next 2 sts) 6 times ....
.... (36 sts)
RND 7: ch 1, (2 dc in next st, 1 dc in next 8 sts) 4 times .... (40 sts)
RND 8: ch 1, 1 dc in BLO of each st ....
.... (40 sts)
RNDS 9-15: ch 1, 1 dc in each st .... (40 sts)
Fasten off, leaving a long tail of yarn for sewing.

VIEWFINDER

Using colour 1, ch 5.
ROW 1: 1 dc in the 2nd ch from the hook and in each ch across, turn .... (4 sts)
ROWS 2-3: ch 1, 1 dc in each st, turn ....
.... (4 sts)
Fasten off, leaving a long tail of yarn for sewing.

DISPLAY SCREEN

Using col 3, ch 14.
ROW 1: 1 dc in the 2nd ch from the hook and in each ch across, turn .... (13 sts)
ROWS 2-10: ch 1, 1 dc in each st, turn ....
.... (13 sts)

Tip

Remember to stuff the camera firmly so that it will keep its shape.

Making the settings dial

Fasten off, leaving a long tail of yarn for sewing.

SETTINGS DIAL

Using col 3, make a magic ring.
RND 1: 6 dc in magic ring, ss to the first st to join.................................... (6 sts)
Insert the safety eye into the centre of the ring with the post facing toward you (the side facing you will be the bottom exterior of the dial) and pull taut to close the circle around the safety eye.
RND 2: ch 1, 2 dc in each st, ss to join .... (12 sts)
RNDS 3-4: ch 1, 1 dc in BLO of each st, ss to

join .... (12 sts)
RND 5: ch 1, dc2tog around, ss to join ....(6 sts)
Fasten off, leaving a yarn tail. Using a yarn needle, thread the tail through the FLO of remaining sts and pull taut to close. Tie off and weave in ends. Use the yarn needle and a bit of contrasting yarn to stitch on dial markings as shown.

SHUTTER BUTTON

Using col 3, make a magic ring.
RND 1: 6 dc in magic circle, ss to the first st to join, and pull taut to close. (6 sts)
Fasten off, leaving a long tail of yarn for sewing.

CAMERA STRAP

Using col 4, leave a long yarn tail at the beginning, ch 4.
ROW 1: 1 dc in 2nd ch from hook and in each ch across, turn .... (3 sts)
ROWS 2-30: ch 1, 1 dc in each st, turn........ ....(3 sts)
Change to col 5.
ROW 31: ch 2, 2 htr in next st, 1 htr in next st, 2 htr in the next st, turn .... (5 sts)
ROW 32: ch 2, 1 htr in each st, turn.... (5 sts)
ROW 33: ch 2, 2 htr in next st, 1 htr in next 3 sts, 2 htr in next st, turn .... (7 sts)
ROWS 34-100: ch 2, 1 htr in each st, turn.... ....(7 sts)
ROW 101: ch 2, htr2tog, 1 htr in next 3 sts, htr2tog, turn .... (5 sts)
ROW 102: ch 2, 1 htr in each st, turn............ ....(5 sts)
ROW 103: ch 2, htr2tog, 1 htr in next st, htr2tog, turn .... (3 sts)

Change to col 4.
ROWS 104-133: ch 1, 1 dc in each st, turn .. (3 sts)
Fasten off, leaving a long tail of yarn for sewing.

CAMERA BODY

Note: Odd numbered rows are RS rows and even numbered rows are WS rows.
Using col 2, ch 13.
ROW 1: 1 dc in 2nd ch from hook and in each ch across, turn..........................(12 sts)
ROWS 2-7: ch 1, 1 dc in each st, turn ....(12 sts)
ROW 8: ch 1, 1 dc in next 11 sts, 2 dc in next st, turn....................................(13 sts)
ROW 9: ch 1, 2 dc in next st, 1 dc in next 12 sts, turn ....(14 sts)
ROW 10: ch 1, 1 dc in next 13 sts, 2 dc in next st, turn....................................(15 sts)
ROW 11: ch 1, 2 dc in next st, 1 dc in next 14 sts, turn ....(16 sts)
ROW 12: ch 1, 1 dc in next 15 sts, 2 dc in next st, turn....................................(17 sts)
ROWS 13-17: ch 1, 1 dc in each st, turn..... ....(17 sts)
ROW 18: ch 1, 1 dc in next 15 sts, dc2tog, turn..(16 sts)
ROW 19: ch 1, dc2tog, 1 dc in next 14 sts, turn..(15 sts)
ROW 20: ch 1, 1 dc in next 13 sts, dc2tog, turn..(14 sts)
ROW 21: ch 1, dc2tog, 1 dc in next 12 sts, turn..(13 sts)
ROW 22: ch 1, 1 dc in next 11 sts, dc2tog, turn..(12 sts)
ROWS 23-26: ch 1, 1 dc in each st, turn.... ....(12 sts)

ROW 27: ch 1, 1 dc in BLO of each st, turn ....(12 sts)

ROWS 28-34: ch 1, 1 dc in each st, turn.... ....(12 sts)

ROW 35: ch 1, 1 dc in BLO of each st, turn (12 sts)

ROWS 36-38: ch 1, 1 dc in each st, turn.... ....(12 sts)

ROW 39: ch 1, 2 dc in next st, 1 dc in next 11 sts, turn ....(13 sts)

ROW 40: ch 1, 1 dc in next 10 sts, 2 dc in next 3 sts, turn ....(16 sts)

ROW 41: ch 1, 2 dc in next 3 sts, 1 dc in next 13 sts, turn ....(19 sts)

ROWS 42-49: ch 1, 1 dc in each st, turn.... ....(19 sts)

ROW 50: ch 1, 1 dc in next 13 sts, dc2tog 3 times, turn....................................(16 sts)

ROW 51: ch 1, dc2tog 3 times, 1 dc in the next 10 sts, turn ....(13 sts)

ROW 52: ch 1,1 dc in next 11 sts, dc2tog, turn..(12 sts)

ROWS 53-55: ch 1, 1 dc in each st, turn..(12 sts)

ROW 56: ch 1, 1 dc in BLO of each st, turn (12 sts)

Note: This should be on the opposite side of the previous BLO rows

ROWS 57-70: ch 1, 1 dc in each st, turn..(12 sts)

Fasten off, leaving a long yarn tail for sewing.

CAMERA BOTTOM

Using col 2, ch 8.

ROW 1: 1 dc 2nd ch from hook and each ch, turn .... (7 sts)

ROWS 2-20: ch 1, 1 dc in each st, turn........ .... (7 sts)

ROW 21: ch 1, 1 dc in next 5 sts, 2 dc in next 2 sts, turn...................................... (9 sts)

ROW 22: ch 1, 2 dc in next 2 sts, 1 dc in next 7 sts, turn.....................................(11 sts)

ROW 23: ch 1, 1 dc in each st, turn .... (11 sts)

ROW 24: ch 1, dc2tog 2 times, 1 dc in next 7 sts, turn................................... (9 sts)

ROW 25: ch 1, 1 dc in next 5 sts, dc2tog twice .... (7 sts)

Fasten off, leaving a long tail for sewing.

CAMERA TOP

Using col 2, ch 8.

ROW 1: 1 dc in 2nd ch from hook and each ch, turn .... (7 sts)

ROWS 2-4: ch 1, 1 dc in each st, turn........... ....(7 sts)

ROW 5: ch 1, 2 dc in next st, 1 dc in next 6 sts, turn.. (8 sts)

ROW 6: ch 1, dc in next 6 sts, 2 dc in the ⇨

next 2 sts, turn.....................................(10 sts)
ROW 7: ch 1, 2 dc in next st, 1 dc in next 9 sts, turn..(11 sts)
ROW 8: ch 1, 1 dc in next 10 sts, 2 dc in next st, turn...(12 sts)
ROWS 9-15: ch 1, 1 dc in each st, turn .... (12 sts)
ROW 16: ch 1, dc in next 10 sts, dc2tog, turn ....(11 sts)
ROW 17: ch 1, dc2tog, 1 dc in next 9 sts, turn ....(10 sts)
ROW 18: ch 1, 1 dc in next 6 sts, dc2tog twice, turn .... (8 sts)
ROW 19: ch 1, dc2tog, 1 dc in next 6 sts, turn ....(7 sts)
ROWS 20-22: ch 1, 1 dc in each st, turn ....(7 sts)
ROW 23: ch 1, 2 dc in next 2 sts, 1 dc in next 5 sts, turn.. (9 sts)
ROW 24: ch 1, 1 dc in next 7 sts, 2 dc in next 2 sts, turn......................................(11 sts)
ROW 25: ch 1, 1 dc in each st, turn .... (11 sts)
ROW 26: ch 1, 1 dc in next 7 sts, dc2tog twice, turn .... (9 sts)
ROW 27: ch 1, dc2tog twice, 1 dc in next 5 sts...(7 sts)
Fasten off, leaving a long tail for sewing.

ASSEMBLY

1 Using a tapestry needle and the long yarn tails, sew the viewfinder and display screen onto the back side of the camera body (the first section you made) as shown. Be sure to sew them on the right side of the camera (the

corners you made with the first two BLO rows will naturally fold, giving you a crisp edge on the right side and a more rounded look on the wrong side). If desired, stitch on decorative buttons using the tapestry needle and a bit of yarn in a contrasting color.

2 Sew the shutter button onto the camera top as shown. Insert the post of the settings dial into the camera top as shown and fasten in place with the backing of the safety eye; the settings dial should now be able to turn 360° while staying securely fastened.

3 Stuff camera lens and sew to the front side of the camera body using the long yarn tail.

4 Optional: Using a matching piece of yarn, make a small stitch starting on the wrong side of the camera body, through the centre of the lens and then pulling the needle back to the wrong side. Pull taut to indent. Fasten off.

5 Sew the body of the camera together along the loose edge to create a tube-like shape.

6 Sew the camera top onto the top of the camera body. It's helpful to use stitch markers or pins to hold the pieces in place while you sew so that everything remains even.

7 Begin stuffing the camera. Sew the camera bottom onto the bottom of the camera body; finish stuffing as you go.

8 Optional to emphasise shape of the rounded grip: Using a matching piece of yarn, make a small stitch starting on the back side of the camera body (the side with the viewfinder and screen) by pulling the needle and yarn through to the front side where the grip begins to protrude and then pulling the needle back to the back of the camera. Pull taut. Repeat as needed across the length of the grip. Fasten off.

9 Sew the camera strap to both sides of the camera, along the top edge. Be sure not to twist the camera strap while you're sewing.

CATCH A TRAIN

PLAYTIME'S NEVER LOOKED SO GOOD

You Will Need...

Yarn:
- 1 x 100g (295m) ball of Wendy Supreme DK (100% acrylic) in:
- Colour 1: Blue (Aster WD34)
- Colour 2: Black (WD40)
- Colour 3: Red (Crimson WD16)
- Colour 4: White (WD01)*

Tools:
- 3.5mm hook (US E/4)
- Yarn needle
- Stitch marker

Other:
- 10 x 15mm buttons; foam in following shapes:
- One 15 x 7.5 x 5.5cm and
- One 7 x 7.5 x 5.5 rectangle for locomotive,
- Two 8 x 7.5 x 5.5cm rectangles for trucks
- Small amount of toy stuffing

LOCOMOTIVE MAIN PART

TOP
With 3.5mm hook and col 1, ch 14.
ROW 1: 1dc in 2nd ch from hook, then 1dc in each ch to end, turn ....(13 sts)
ROWS 2-28: ch 1 (does not count as a st throughout), 1dc in each st, turn ....
....(13 sts)

SIDES
RND 1: ch 1, 1 dc in next 12 sts, 3 dc in last st, work 2 3dc evenly along row-ends of top, 3 dc in corner, 1 dc in each of next 11ch, 3dc in next corner, work 23 dc evenly along other row-ends, 2 dc in same st as first dc, sl st in back loop of first dc   (80 sts)
RND 2: ch 1, 1 dc in same place as sl st, 1 dc in BLO of each st to end, sl st in first dc (80 sts)
RND 3: ch 2 (counts as 1htr), 1 htr in each st....................................... (80 sts)
Mark end of last round and move marker up at end of every round.
RNDS 4-5: 1htr in each st. Join col 2 and slst in first st   (80 sts)
RND 6: With col 2, ch 1, 1 dc in each st to end, join in col 3 and sl st in back loop of first dc .... (80 sts)
RND 7: With col 3, ch 1, 1 dc in same place as slst, 1 dc in BLO of each st to end .... (80 sts)
RNDS 8-10: 1 dc in BLO of each st to end (80 sts)
Sl st in first dc. Fasten off.

BASE
With 3.5mm hook and col 3, ch 14.
Work ROWS 1-28 as given for top.
Fasten off.

Lining up corners with those of top, sew base along lower edge of sides, leaving one long side open. Insert larger locomotive foam piece and close opening.

CAB

TOP
With 3.5mm hook and col 1, ch 14.

ROW 1: 1 dc in 2nd ch from hook, 1 dc in each ch, turn ....(13 sts)
ROWS 2-12: ch 1 (does not count as a st throughout), 1 dc in each st, turn ....
....(13 sts)

SIDES
RND 1: 1 dc in next 12 sts, 3 dc in last st, work 9 dc evenly along row-ends of top, 3 dc in corner, 1dc in next 11 sts, 3 dc in next corner, work 9 dc evenly along other row-ends, 2 dc in same st as first dc, sl st in back loop of first dc.................... (52 sts)
RND 2: ch 1, 1 dc in same place as sl st, 1 dc in BLO of each st to end, sl st in first dc (52 sts)
RND 3: ch 2 (counts as 1 htr), 1 htr in each st to end... (52 sts)
Mark end of last round and move marker up at end of every round.
RNDS 4-8: 1 htr in each st.........(52 sts)
Sl st in first st. Fasten off.
Insert remaining locomotive foam piece in cab and place base on top of main part, then sew in position.

ROOF
With 3.5mm hook and col 2, ch 15.
ROW 1: 1 dc in 2nd ch from hook, 1dc in each ch to end, turn ....(14 sts)
ROWS 2-14: ch 1, 1 dc in each st, turn ......
....(14 sts)

EDGING ROUND: 1 dc in next 13 sts, 3 dc in last st, work 11 dc evenly along row-ends of roof, 3 dc in corner, 1 dc in each of 12ch, 3 dc in next corner, work 11 dc evenly along other row-ends, 2 dc in same st as first dc, sl st in first dc . (58 sts) Fasten off.
Place roof on top of cab, allowing edging to overhang all round, stitch in position.

WINDOW PANE

With 3.5mm hook and col 4, ch 14.
ROW 1: 1 dc in 2nd ch from hook, 1 dc in each ch to end, turn ....(13 sts)
ROWS 2-10: ch 1, 1 dc in each st, turn ......
....(13 sts)
Fasten off.
Frame: With 3.5mm hook, col 1 and working through fabric slightly away from edges, work 1 round of ch sts around window pane. Fasten off.
Place window at front of cab and stitch in position.

WHEELS

(Make 6)
RND 1: With 3.5mm hook and Black, make slip ring as follows: wind yarn round index finger of left hand to form ring, insert hook into ring, yarn over hook and pull through, ch 1, work 6 dc in ring, pull end of yarn tightly to close ring.
Mark end of last round and move marker up at end of every round.
RND 2: 2 dc in each st......................(12 sts)
RND 3: (1 dc in next st, 2 dc in next st) 6 times.....................................(18 sts)
RND 4: 1 dc in next st, 2 dc in next st, then (1 dc in next 2 sts, 2 dc in next st] 5 times, 1 dc in last st, slst in back loop of first dc .... (24 sts)
RND 5: ch 1, 1 dc in same place as slst, 1 dc in BLO of next 23 sts, sl st in back loop of first dc .... (24 sts)
RND 6: Working in BLO of every st, 1 dc in same place as sl st, 1 dc in next st, dc2tog, then (1 dc in next 2 sts, dc2tog) 5 times, sl st in first dc.......................(18 sts)
RND 7: ch 1, 1 dc in same place as sl st, dc2tog, then (1 dc in next st, dc2tog) 5 times.....................................(12 sts)
RND 8: dc2tog 6 times ....(6 sts)
Fasten off.
Stuff each wheel lightly, flatten and join opening, then sew button to centre front. Position and sew 3 wheels at each side of main part.

CHIMNEY

Work RNDS 1-5 as given for wheels.
RND 6: ch 1, 1 dc in same place as sl st, 1 dc in next st, dc2tog, then (1 dc in next 2 sts, dc2tog) 5 times, join col 1 and sl st in first st ....(18 sts)
RND 7: ch 1, 1 dc in each st.............(18 sts)
RND 8: 1 dc in each st.....................(18 sts)
RND 9: (1 dc in next 4 sts, dc2tog) 3 times...(15 sts)
RND 10: 1 dc in each st...................(15 sts)
Fasten off.
Rim round: Rejoin Black to any loop on 4th round, ch 1, 1 dc in same place as join, 1 dc in next loop 23 times, slst in first dc. Fasten off.
Stuff chimney firmly and place open end on top at front of main part and sew in position.

FIRST TRUCK

TOP

With 3.5mm hook and col 2, ch 14.
ROW 1: 1 dc in 2nd ch from hook, 1 dc in each ch to end, turn ....(13 sts)
ROWS 2-14: ch 1 (does not count as a st throughout), 1 dc in each st, turn ....
....(13 sts)

SIDES

RND 1: 1 dc in next 12 sts, 3 dc in last st, work 11 dc evenly along row-ends of top, 3 dc in corner, 1 dc in each of next 11ch, 3 dc in next corner, work 11 dc evenly along other row-ends, 2 dc in same st as first dc, sl st in back loop of first dc ...... (56 sts)
RND 2: ch 1, 1 dc in same place as sl st, 1 dc in BLO of each st to end, slst in first dc (56 sts)
RND 3: ch 2 (counts as 1htr throughout), 1 htr in each st to end, join in col 1 and slst in top of 2ch...
.... (56 sts)
RND 5: ch 2, 1htr in each st   (56 sts)
Mark end of last round and move marker up at end of every round.
RNDS 6-8: 1 htr in each st.............. (56 sts)
Slst in first st. Fasten off.

SIDE RAIL

RND 1: Rejoin col 2 to any loop on 1st round of sides, ch 2, 1htr in next 55 loops, sl st in top of 2ch .... (56 sts)
RND 2: ch 2, 1 htr in next 55 sts, sl st in top of 2ch... (56 sts)
Fasten off.
Base: With 3.5mm hook and col 1,

ch 14.
Work ROWS 1-14 as given for top of main part. Fasten off.
Lining up corners with those of top, sew base along lower edge of sides, leaving one side open. Insert foam piece and close opening.

WHEELS

(Make 2)
Work as given for wheels of locomotive. Stuff each wheel lightly, flatten and join opening, then sew button to centre front. Position and sew one wheel at each side of truck.

SECOND TRUCK

MAIN PART

Using col 3 instead of col 2, work as main part of first truck.

WHEELS

(Make 2)
Work as given for wheels of locomotive. Stuff each wheel lightly, flatten and join opening, then sew button to centre front. Position and sew one wheel at each side of truck.

CONNECTERS

(Make 2)
With 3.5mm hook and col 2, ch 5, sl st in first ch to form ring.
RND 1: 1 dc in same place as sl st, 1 dc in each ch.. (5 sts)
RND 2-8: 1 dc in each st .... (5 sts)
Slst in next st. Fasten off.
Attach one end of first connecter to back of locomotive and the other end to front of first truck. Attach one end of second connecter to back of first truck and the other end to front of second truck.

Pattern

Finished product size: approx. Locomotive: Approx 16cm/6¼in long, 8cm/3in wide and 13cm/5in high. Truck: Approx 9cm/3½in long, 8cm/3in wide and 7cm/2¾in high.

* **NOTE:** Yarn amounts are based on average requirements and are therefore approximate. Instructions in brackets are worked as stated after 2nd bracket.

Pattern by:

Anneris Kondratas

Anneris is an illustrator and a crochet designer who lives in Virginia with her husband and two sons. Everything started as a hobby, writing a blog about food characters that she called Amigurumi Food. Since 2015 she has been selling her creations and patterns on Etsy.

@amigurumifood
www.etsy.com/shop/Amigurumifood

You Will Need...

Yarn:

- You will need to use aran weight yarn in your chosen colours. We have used Lion Brand Vanna's Choice in:
- Colour 1: Red
- Colour 2: White
- Colour 3: Brown
- Colour 4: Light yellow
- Colour 5: Green
- Colour 6: Soft white
- Colour 7: Cornmeal yellow
- Colour 8: Rust
- Colour 9: Beige
- Colour 10: Light brown
- Colour 11: Golden
- Colour 12: Lime
- Colour 13: Purple
- Colour 14: Honey

Tools:

- 2.75mm or 3mm hook (US C/2)
- Embroidery needle
- Embroidery thread in pink, black, green and white
- Fibrefill stuffing
- Stitch marker
- Yarn needle
- Two 6mm black toy safety eyes for each item

AMIGURUMI FOOD

THIS SET IS THE PERFECT TREAT FOR ANY CHILD – AND THE PIECES WORK UP QUICKLY, TOO

Pattern

Finished product size: Mini soda fresh cola: 15cm (6in) Ketchup: 12cm (4¾in) Mini hot dog: 10cm (4in) Mini burger: 9cm (3½in) Mini toast: 8cm (3in)

★ **SPECIAL STITCHES**

Crab stitch: worked as a regular dc stitch, but working into the stitch to the right of your hook, rather than the left. Chain stitch (embroidery): Insert the embroidery needle from the back and pull thread through. * Re-insert the needle through the fabric as if to make one small running stitch (and bringing the needle out just a short distance along), then place the thread behind the needle. Pull the needle through to create a chain stitch (do not pull too tightly – leave the thread loose). To continue the chain, rep from *, each time inserting the needle back into same place and out again a little further along. Keep going as needed.

★ **NOTES** ■ Most pieces are worked in a spiral, without joining each round. It may help to use a stitch marker to mark the first stitch of the round, and move it up as you work each round.
■ To change colour in last st of rnd, work your stitch until there are two loops left on hook, drop yarn and work the last yoh in new colour and pull a loop through. New colour is on hook, ready to start next rnd in that colour.

MINI SODA FRESH COLA

BOTTLE

Using col 3, make a magic ring.
RND 1 (RS): 6 dc in magic ring and pull ring tight to close...........................(6 sts)
RND 2: 2 dc in each st ....(12 sts)
RND 3: (1 dc in next st, 2 dc in next st) 6 times...(18 sts)
RND 4: (1 dc in next 2 sts, 2 dc in next st) 6 times....................................(24 sts)
RND 5: (1 dc in next 3 sts, 2 dc in next st) 6 times....................................(30 sts)
RND 6: 1 dc in back loop of each st. ....
....(30 sts)
RND 7: 1 dc in each st ....(30 sts)
RND 8: (1 dc in next 3 sts, dc2tog) 6 times..(24 sts)
RND 9: 1 dc in each st ....(24 sts)
RND 10: (1 dc in next 2 sts, dc2tog) 6 times..(18 sts)
RND 11: (1 dc in next 2 sts, 2 dc in ⇨

next st) 6 times.............................(24 sts)
RND 12: (1 dc in next 3 sts, 2 dc in next st) 6 times.....................................(30 sts)
In last st of last rnd, change to col 1.
RND 13: 1 dc in each st. ....(30 sts)
In last st of last rnd, change to col 2.
RND 14: 1 dc in each st. ....(30 sts)
In last st of last rnd, change to col 1.
RNDS 15-18: 1 dc in each st ....(30 sts)
Place safety eyes between RNDS 16-17.
Embroider cheeks on each side of eyes, by making three horizontal backstitches with pink thread.
Embroider mouth beneath the eyes, by making two diagonal backstitches with black thread.
Change to col 2.
RND 19: 1 dc in each st ....(30 sts)
In last st of last rnd, change to col 1.
RND 20: 1 dc in each st. ....(30 sts)
In last st of last rnd, change to col 3.
RND 21: (1 dc in next 3 sts, dc2tog) 6 times.....................................(24 sts)
RND 22: 1 dc in each st ....(24 sts)
RND 23: (1 dc in next 2 sts, dc2tog) 6 times..(18 sts)
Fill the bottle with fibrefill stuffing.
RND 24: (1 dc in next st, dc2tog) 6

times...(12 sts)
RND 25: 1 dc in each st. ....(12 sts)
In last st of last rnd, change to col 2.
RND 26: 1 dc in each st ....(12 sts)
RND 27: 1 crab stitch in each st ....
....(12 sts)
Sl st in first st and fasten off.

STRAW

Using col 2, make a magic ring.
RND 1 (RS): 6 dc in magic ring and pull tight to close ....(6 sts)
RNDS 2-5: 1 dc in each st..............(6 sts)
In last st of last rnd, change to col 4.
RNDS 6-9: 1 dc in each st..............(6 sts)
In last st of last rnd, change to col 2.
RND 10: 1 dc in each st. ....(6 sts)
Sl st in next st and fasten off, leaving a long tail for sewing. No stuffing is needed.

ASSEMBLY

Place the straw inside the bottle, following the position with the photo tutorial. Sew RND 10 of the straw to RND 26 of the bottle.

KETCHUP

LABEL

Using col 2, ch 4.
RND 1: 2 dc in 2nd chain from hook, 1 dc in next ch, 4 dc in last ch, rotate and work along the opposite side of the chains, 1 dc in next ch, 2 dc in last ch.....
...................................(10 sts)
Continue to work in a spiral.
RND 2: 2 dc in first st, 2 dc in next st, 1 dc in next st, 2 dc in next 4 sts, 1 dc in next st, 2 dc in next 2 sts. ....(18 sts)
Sl st in next st and fasten off, leaving a long tail for sewing.
Embroider a chain stitch around the edge of the label with green thread.
Place the safety eyes in the centre and embroider the mouth with black thread.

BOTTLE

Using col 1, make a magic ring.
RND 1 (RS): 6 dc in magic ring and pull tight to close ....(6 sts)
RND 2: 2 dc in each st. ....(12 sts)
RND 3: (1 dc in next st, 2 dc in next st) 6 times..(18 sts)
RND 4: (1 dc in next 2 sts, 2 dc in next

st) 6 times......................................(24 sts)
RND 5: (1 dc in next 3 sts, 2 dc in next st) 6 times.................................(30 sts)
RND 6: 1 dc in back loop of each st..(30 sts)
RND 7-16: 1 dc in each st. ....(30 sts)
RND 17: (1 dc in next 3 sts, dc2tog) 6 times..(24 sts)
RND 18: 1 dc in each st ....(24 sts)
RND 19: (1 dc in next 2 sts, dc2tog) 6 times.. (18 sts)
Sew the label between RNDS 14 and 18.
RNDS 20-21: 1 dc in each st. (18 sts)
RND 22: (1 dc in next st, dc2tog) 6 times...(12 sts)
Place the fibrefill stuffing inside the piece.
RND 23: 1 dc in each st. ....(12 sts)
In last st of last rnd, change to col 2.
RND 24: 1 dc in each st .... (12 sts)
In last st of last rnd, change to col 5.
RND 25: 1 dc in each st .... (12 sts)
In last st of last rnd, change to col 1.
RNDS 26-27: 1 dc in each st........(12 sts)
RND 28: 1 dc in back loop of each st...(12 sts)
RND 29: (dc2tog) 6 times. ....(6 sts)
Sl st in next st and fasten off.

TOP

Using col 2, make a magic ring.
RND 1 (RS): 6 dc in magic ring and pull

tight to close ....(6 sts)
RND 2: 2 dc in each st ....(12 sts)
RND 3: 1 dc in back loop of each st...(12 sts)
RND 4: Sl st in each st ....(12 sts)
Fasten off.

ASSEMBLY
Sew the top to the bottle.

MINI HOT DOG

OUTSIDE BUN
(Make 2)
Using col 7, ch 15.
RND 1 (RS): 2 dc in 2nd chain from hook, 1 dc in next 12 sts, 3 dc in last st, rotate and work along opposite side of chains, 1 dc in next 12 ch, 1 dc in last ch (30 sts)
Continue to work in a spiral.
RND 2: 2 dc in first st, 2 dc in next st, 1 dc in next 12 sts, 2 dc in next 3 sts, 1 dc in next 12 sts, 2 dc in last st....................
....(36 sts)
RNDS 3-4: 1 dc in each st......................
....(36 sts)

Sl st in next st, fasten off and leave a long tail for sewing.

INSIDE BUN
(Make 2)
Using col 6, ch 15.
RND 1 (RS): 2 dc in 2nd chain from hook, 1 dc in next 12 ch, 3 dc in last ch, rotate and work along opposite side of chains, 1 dc in next 12 ch, 1 dc in last ch (30 sts)
Continue to work in a spiral.
RND 2: 2 dc in first st, 2 dc in next st, 1 dc in next 12 sts, 2 dc in next 3 sts, 1 dc in next 12 sts, 2 dc in last st...................
....(36 sts)

Sl st in next st and fasten off.

HOT DOG
Using col 8, make a magic ring.
RND 1 (RS): 6 dc in magic ring and pull tight to close ....(6 sts)
RND 2: 2 dc in each st ....(12 sts)
RNDS 3-7: 1 dc in each st ....(12 sts)
Place safety eyes in RND 6. Embroider mouth and cheeks with black and pink thread.
RNDS 8-19: 1 dc in each st. ....(12 sts)

Stuff with fibrefill stuffing.
RND 20: (dc2tog) 6 times..............(6 sts)

ASSEMBLY

1 Sew the two buns together, right sides facing out. For the ketchup swirl, ch 20 in col 1, leaving a long tail.

2 Sew the strip of ketchup to the hot dog in a zigzag pattern.

3 Using col 7, secure the hot dog between the buns.

MINI BURGER

OUTSIDE BUN

(Make 2)
Using col 9, make a magic ring.
RND 1 (RS): 6 dc in magic ring and pull tight to close ....(6 sts)
RND 2: 2 dc in each st .... (12 sts)
RND 3: (1 dc in next st, 2 dc in next st) 6 times..(18 sts)
RND 4: (1 dc in next st, 2 dc in next st) 6 times..(24 sts)
RND 5: (1 dc in next 3 sts, 2 dc in next st) 6 times..................................(30 sts)
RND 6: (1 dc in next 4 sts, 2 dc in next st) 6 times..................................(36 sts)
RNDS 7-8: 1 dc in each st............(36 sts)
Sl st in next st and fasten off, leaving a long tail for sewing.
Place safety eyes in RND 6, leaving a small gap in between them. Embroider mouth with black thread making two diagonal backstitches. Embroider cheeks with pink thread by making 3 horizontal backstitches. Embroider sesame seeds on top of the bun by making one backstitch with double thread in warm yellow.

INSIDE BUN

(Make 2)
Using col 6, make a magic ring.
RND 1 (RS): 6 dc in magic ring and pull tight to close ....(6 sts)
RND 2: 2 dc in each st .... (12 sts)
RND 3: (1 dc in next st, 2 dc in next st) 6 times..(18 sts)
RND 4: (1 dc in next st, 2 dc in next st) 6 times..(24 sts)
RND 5: (1 dc in next 3 sts, 2 dc in next st) 6 times..................................(30 sts)
RND 6: (1 dc in next 4 sts, 2 dc in next st) 6 times..................................(36 sts)

Sl st in next st and fasten off.

BURGER PATTY

Using col 10, make magic ring.
RND 1 (RS): 6 dc in magic ring and pull tight to close ....(6 sts)
RND 2: 2 dc in each st .... (12 sts)
RND 3: (1 dc in next st, 2 dc in next st) 6 times..(18 sts)
RND 4: (1 dc in next st, 2 dc in next st) 6 times..(24 sts)
RND 5: (1 dc in next 3 sts, 2 dc in next st) 6 times..................................(30 sts)
RND 6: (1 dc in next 4 sts, 2 dc in next st) 6 times..................................(36 sts)
RND 7: 1 dc in each st ....(36 sts)
RND 8: (1 dc in next 4 sts, dc2tog) 6 times..(30 sts)
RND 9: (1 dc in next 3 sts, dc2tog) 6 times..(24 sts)
RND 10: (1 dc in next 2 sts, dc2tog) 6 times..(18 sts)
RND 11: (1 dc in next st, dc2tog) 6 times (12 sts)
RND 12: (dc2tog) 6 times ....(6 sts)
Sl st in next st and fasten off. No stuffing is needed.

LETTUCE

Using col 12, make a magic ring.
RND 1 (RS): 6 dc in magic ring and pull tight to close ....(6 sts)
RND 2: 2 dc in each st .... (12 sts)
RND 3: (1 dc in next st, 2 dc in next st) 6 times..(18 sts)
RND 4: (1 dc in next 2 sts, 2 dc in next st) 6 times..................................(24 sts)
RND 5: (1 dc in next 3 sts, 2 dc in next st) 6 times..................................(30 sts)
RND 6: (1 dc in next 4 sts, 2 dc in next st) 6 times..................................(36 sts)
RND 7: *(1 tr and 1 dtr) in next st, (1 dtr and 1 tr) in next st, sl st in next st; rep from * 11 times more ....(60 sts)
Fasten off and weave in ends.

CHEESE

Using col 11, ch 12.
ROW 1: 1 dc in 2nd chain from hook, 1 dc in each of next 10 ch, turn ....
.... (11 sts)
ROWS 2-8: Ch 1 (does not count as a st), 1 dc in each st to end, turn ....
.... (11 sts)
Do not fasten off, continue to work a

border around the cheese, by working 1 dc in same st (to make a corner), work 1 dc in each st or row-end and 2 dc in each corner, then when you reach the end, sl st in first dc and fasten off.

TOMATO SLICE

Using col 1, make a magic ring.
RND 1 (RS): 6 dc in magic ring and pull tight to close ....(6 sts)
RND 2: 2 dc in each st ....(12 sts)
RND 3: (1 dc in next st, 2 dc in next st) 6 times..(18 sts)
RND 4: (1 dc in next 2 sts, 2 dc in next st) 6 times.....................................(24 sts)
RND 5: (1 dc in next 3 sts, 2 dc in next st) 6 times.....................................(30 sts)
RND 6: Sl st in first st, ch 3 (counts as first tr), 1 tr in next 3 sts, ch 2, skip 1 st, (1 tr in next 4 sts, ch 2, skip 1 st) 5 times. Sl st to top of beginning ch 3 and fasten off .... (30 tr and 6 ch2-sps)

ASSEMBLY

1 Sew the two buns together, with right sides facing out.

2 Stuff with fibrefill before closing.

3 Sew all of the pieces together using col 9, through the middle of each one in the following order:
- Bottom bun
- Lettuce
- Tomato
- Burger
- Cheese
- Top bun

4 Secure all parts to the top bun.

TOAST

(Make 2)
Using col 9, ch 13.
ROW 1 (RS): 1 dc in 2nd chain from hook, 1 dc in next 11 ch, turn ....(12 sts)
ROWS 2-10: Ch 1 (does not count as a st throughout), 1 dc in each st to end, turn..(12 sts)
ROW 11: Ch 1, 2 dc in first st, 1 dc in each st to last st, 2 dc in last st, turn. ....(14 sts)
ROW 12: As Row 11 ....(16 sts)
ROW 13: As Row 11 but do not turn at end ....(18 sts)

Fasten off.
With RS facing, join col 14 with a sl st to last st, and ch 1.
Edging rnd: 2 dc in same st, then work dc around the edge of the toast, by working 1 dc in each st or row-end and 2 dc in each corner. Sl st in first dc and fasten off, leaving a long tail for sewing.

JELLY/PEANUT BUTTER

Using col 13 (for jelly) or col 11 (for peanut butter), make a magic ring.
RND 1 (RS): 6 dc in magic ring and pull tight to close ....(6 sts)
RND 2: 2 dc in each st ....(12 sts)
RND 3: (2 tr in next 4 sts, sl st in same st as last 2 tr) twice, 2 htr in next 4 sts, sl st in same st as last 2 htr, sl st in top of first tr.
Fasten off, leaving a long tail for sewing.

ASSEMBLY

1 Place safety eyes between RNDS 1 and 2 of the jelly/peanut butter part.

2 Embroider cheeks with pink and mouth with white thread.

3 Sew the jelly and peanut butter to one slice of toast.

4 Place and sew the slices of toast together working with col 10 and 14 through the edge.

BABY ROBOT

A CUTE ANDROID THAT'S PERFECT FOR PLAYTIME

Pattern by:

Tetiana Saienko

Tetiana is the amigurumi designer behind Planet Piu. She lives in Ukraine. Her amigurumi passion started in 2013, and now she creates her own amigurumi patterns and shares her creative processes on her website and socials. She loves to meet so many wonderful people from all over the world!

planet-piu.com

You Will Need...

Yarn:
- You will need to use sport (4ply) weight yarn in your chosen colours. Here we have used a variety of brands in:
- Colour 1: White
- Colour 2: Light Blue
- Colour 3: Grey
- Colour 4: Red (optional)
- Colour 5: Yellow (optional)
- Colour 6: Light Green (optional)

Tools:
- 1.5mm hook
- Yarn needle
- Scissors

Other:
- Fibrefill
- A pair of 8mm safety eyes

Pattern

Finished product size: 19-20cm (7.5-7.9in) tall, without antenna

* **ADDITIONAL STITCH: Fastening slip stitch (fst sl st):** Fastening slip stitch appears the same as a slip stitch, but is not crocheted. The stitch is made with a needle and gives an even edge at the end of a row while fastening the thread. Insert the end of a thread, left after crocheting the detail, in a needle. Insert needle from the front to the back through both loops in a stitch next to the last crocheted stitch. Pull tight. Insert needle from front to back in the back loop of the last crocheted stitch in a row. Pull tight.

FACE SCREEN
Using col 2, ch 11.
RND 1: 2 dc in 2nd ch from hook, 1 dc in next 8 chs, 4 dc in last ch, then, working along the other side of the ch, 1 dc in next 8 chs, 2 dc in last ch..(24 sts)
RND 2: 2 dc in next st, 1 dc in next 9 sts, 2 dc in next 3 sts, 1 dc in next 9 sts, 2 dc in next 2 sts ....(30 sts)
RND 3: 1 dc in next st, 2 dc in next st, 1 dc in next 10 sts, 2 dc in next st, then (1 dc in next st, 2 dc in next st) 2 times, 1 dc in next 10 sts, 2 dc in next st, 1 dc in next st, 2 dc in next st...(36 sts)
RND 4 1 dc in next 2 sts, 2 dc in next st, 1 htr in next 11 sts, 2 dc in next st, then (1 dc in next 2 sts, 2 dc in next st) 2 times, 1 htr in next 11 sts, 2 dc in next st, 1 dc in next 2 sts, 2 dc in next st . (42 sts)
RND 5: 1 htr in next 3 sts, 2 htr in next st, 1 tr in next 12 sts, 2 htr in next st, 1 htr in next 7 sts, 2 htr in next st, 1 tr in next 12 sts, 2 htr in next st, 1 htr in next 4 sts ....(46 sts)
RND 6: 2 dc in next st, 2 dc in next st, change to col 1, 1 sl st, 2 dc in next st, 1 dc in next 13 sts, 2 dc in next st, 1 dc in next 8 sts, 2 dc in next st, 1 dc in next 13 sts, 2 dc in next st, 1 dc in next 4 sts (50 sts)
RND 7: 1 dc in next 4 sts, sl st. Fasten off, leaving long tail for sewing.

Place safety eyes between rnds 1 and 2, under the 1st and 10th sts of the foundation ch. Do not put the washers on – this will be done later. ⇨

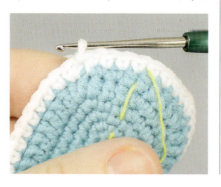

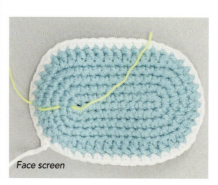
Face screen

Crochet TOYBOX

HEAD

Using col 1, ch 8.

RND 1: 2 dc in 2nd ch from hook, 1 dc in next 5 chs, 4 dc in last ch, then, working along the other side of the ch, 1 dc in next 5 chs, 2 dc in last ch........... .... (18 sts)

RND 2: 2 dc in next st, 1 dc in next 6 sts, 2 dc in next 3 sts, 1 dc in next 6 sts, 2 dc in next 2 sts .... (24 sts)

RND 3: 1 dc in next st, 2 dc in next st, 1 dc in next 7 sts, 2 dc in next st, then (1 dc in next st, 2 dc in next st) 2 times, 1 dc in next 7 sts, 2 dc in next st, 1 dc in next st, 2 dc in next st.............................. ....(30 sts)

RND 4: 1 dc in next 2 sts, 2 dc in next st, 1 dc in next 8 sts, 2 dc in next st, then (1 dc in next 2 sts, 2 dc in next st) 2 times, 1 dc in next 8 sts, 2 dc in next st, 1 dc in next 2 sts, 2 dc in next st (36 sts)

RND 5: 1 dc in next 3 sts, 2 dc in next st, 1 dc in next 9 sts, 2 dc in next st, then (1 dc in next 3 sts, 2 dc in next st) 2 times, 1 dc in next 9 sts, 2 dc in next st, 1 dc in next 3 sts, 2 dc in next st (42 sts)

RND 6: (1 dc in next 13 sts, 2 dc in next st) 3 times.................................(45 sts)

Rnd 7: 1 dc in next 7 sts, 2 dc in next st, then (1 dc in next 14 sts, 2 dc in next st) 2 times, 1 dc in next 7 sts......................... ....(48 sts)

RND 8: (1 dc in next 15 sts, 2 dc in next st) 3 times.................................. (51 sts)

RND 9: 1 dc in next 8 sts, 2 dc in next st, then (1 dc in next 16 sts, 2 dc in next st) 2 times, 1 dc in next 8 sts ....(54 sts)

RND 10: (1 dc in next 17 sts, 2 dc in next st) 3 times...........................(57 sts)

RND 11: 1 dc in next 9 sts, 2 dc in next st, then (1 dc in next 18 sts, 2 dc in next st) 2 times, 1 dc in next 9 sts ....(60 sts)

RND 12: (1 dc in next 14 sts, 2 dc in next st) 4 times................................(64 sts)

RNDS 13-20: 1 dc in each st.......(64 sts) Work 1 dc in next 16 sts. Move stitch marker to last st.

RND 21: 1 dc in next 3 sts, dc2tog, then (1 dc in next 6 sts, dc2tog) 7 times, 1 dc in next 3 sts................................(56 sts)

RND 22: (1 dc in next 5 sts, dc2tog) 8 times...(48 sts)

Keeping the safety eyes in the face screen, now insert them between RNDS 16 and 17 of the head.

You can use pins before inserting them to make sure everything is symmetrical. Once inserted, fix them in place with the washers.

Continue crocheting, bending the face slightly forward for a while and stuffing the head as you go.

How your eyes should look in the head

Close up the hole at the top of the head

RND 24: 1 dc in next 2 sts, dc2tog, then (1 dc in next 4 sts, dc2tog) 7 times, 1 dc in next 2 sts ....(40 sts)

RND 25: (1 dc in next 3 sts, dc2tog) 8 times...(32 sts)

RND 26: 1 dc in next st, dc2tog, then (1 dc in next 2 sts, dc2tog) 7 times, 1 dc in next st...(24 sts)

RND 27: In BLO, (1 dc in next 2 sts, dc2tog) 6 times............................ (18 sts) Stuff head completely.

RND 28: (1 dc in next st, dc2tog) 6 times..(12 sts)

RND 29: dc2tog 6 times...............(6 sts) Fasten off, leaving long tail. Tighten the left 6 sts through the front loops only, then weave in ends.

Sew the face to the head using fastening sl st. Finish off and weave in ends.

EARS

Central part (make 2)

Using col 2, make magic ring.

RND 1: 6 dc in magic ring............(6 sts)

RND 2: 2 dc in each st ....(12 sts)

RND 3: (1 dc in next st, 2 dc in next st) 6 times...(18 sts)

RND 4: (1 dc in next 5 sts, 2 dc in next st) 3 times....................................(21 sts)

Fasten off.

Main part (make 2)

Using col 1, make magic ring,

RND 1: 7 dc in magic ring.............(7 sts)

RND 2: 2 dc in each st ....(14 sts)

RND 3: (1 dc in next st, 2 dc in next st) 7 times...(21 sts)

Do not finish off.

Place both parts of the ear together with the wrong sides facing each other. The central part should be on top.

Sewing the ear parts together

Crochet RND 4 through both loops of the main part and back loops of the central part (loops closest to you) together. Stuff lightly as you go.

RND 4: 1 dc in next st, 2 dc in next st, then (1 dc in next 2 sts, 2 dc in next st) 6 times, 1 dc in next st...................(28 sts)
Now continue on the main part only.
RND 5: (1 dc in next 3 sts, 2 dc in next st) 7 times....................................(35 sts)
RND 6: In BLO, 1 dc in each st ...(35 sts)
RND 7: dc2tog, 1 dc on next st, dc2tog) 7 times...(21 sts)
Crochet 21 sl st through both loops of the main part and left free loops of the central part together. Do not stuff. Finish off, leaving long tail for sewing. Make 1 fst sl st and weave in ends.

BIG STRIPE ON THE HEAD
Using col 2, ch 9.
RND 1: 2 dc in 2nd ch from hook, 1 dc in next 6 chs, 4 dc in last ch, then, working along other side of the ch, 1 dc in next 6 chs, 2 dc in last ch...................
....(20 sts)
RND 2: 2 dc in next st, 1 dc in next 7 sts, 2 dc in next 3 sts, 1 dc in next 7 sts, 2 dc in next 2 sts ....(26 sts)
RND 3: 1 dc in next st, 2 dc in next st, 1 dc in next 8 sts, 2 dc in next st, then (1 dc in next st, 2 dc in next st) 2 times, 1 dc in next 8 sts, 2 dc in next st, 1 dc in next st, 2 dc in next st.................(32 sts)
RND 4: 1 dc in next 2 sts, 2 dc in next st, 1 dc in next 9 sts, 2 dc in next st, then (1 dc in next 2 sts, 2 dc in next st) 2 times, 1 dc in next 9 sts, 2 dc in next st, 1 dc in next 2 sts, 2 dc in next st ....
....(38 sts)
RND 5: 1 dc in next 2 sts, change to col 1, 1 sl st, 1 dc in next 12 sts, 2 dc in next st, 1 dc in next 4 sts, 2 dc in next st, 1

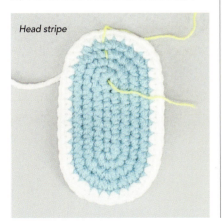

Head stripe

dc in next 13 sts, 2 dc in next st, 1 dc in next 3 sts......................................(42 sts)
RND 6: 1 dc in next st, 2 dc in next st, 1 dc in next st, sl st.
Finish off, leaving long tail, and make 1 fst sl st.

Now you can choose what look you want to create for your robot – an antenna or a small stripe on the head.

ANTENNA
Stuff as you go.
Using col 1, make magic ring.
RND 1: 6 dc in magic ring.............(6 sts)
RND 2: 2 dc in each st .... (12 sts)
RND 3: 1 dc in each st .... (12 sts)
RND 4: dc2tog 6 times.................(6 sts)
Change to col 2.
RNDS 5-6: 1 dc in each st.............(6 sts)
Sl st and finish off, leaving long tail.

Antenna

SMALL STRIPE ON THE HEAD
Using col 1, ch 9.
RND 1: 2 dc in 2nd ch from hook, 1 dc in next 6 chs, 4 dc in last ch, then, working along other side of ch, 1 dc in next 6 chs, 2 dc in last ch............(20 sts)
RND 2: 2 dc in next st, 1 dc in next 7 sts, 2 dc in next 3 sts, 1 dc in next 7 sts, 2 dc in next 2 sts ....(26 sts)
Work 1 dc in next st and then sl st. Fasten off leaving long tail for sewing, and make 1 fst sl st.

HEAD ASSEMBLY
1 Attach the ears to the head with pins between rows 9 and 20. The distance between the edge of the face and the ear is 1-2 sts. Make sure that ears are placed symmetrically. Sew to the head by grabbing the left free loops along the edges of the ears. Do not stuff.
Fasten off and weave in ends.

2 Sewing on a big stripe
Attach the big stripe to the head with pins. The distance between the upper edge of the face and the front edge of the stripe is 2-3 rounds. The back edge of the stripe should be between rnds 9-11 of the back of the head. Make sure the stripe is centred. Sew the stripe to the head in the same ⇨

Pin your ear pieces together before sewing

Attaching the head stripe and antenna

way as for the face. Do not stuff. Finish off and weave in ends.

3 Sewing on an antenna
Attach the antenna to the head with pins exactly in the centre of the top of the head. Sew the antenna to the head.
Finish off and weave in ends.

4 Sewing on a small stripe
Attach the small stripe to the head with pins exactly on top of the big stripe. Sew the stripe in the same way as for the face. In the process of sewing you can stuff the stripe a bit if you wish, or leave it flat.
Finish off and weave in ends.

BODY
Using col 1, ch 12.
RND 1: 2 dc in 2nd ch from hook, 1 dc in next 9 chs, 4 dc in last ch, then, working along other side of the ch, 1 dc in next 9 chs, 2 dc in last ch .... (26 sts)
RND 2: 2 dc in next 2 sts, 1 dc in next 9 sts, 2 dc in next 4 sts, 1 dc in next 9 sts, 2 dc in next 2 sts .... (34 sts)

RNDS 3-14: 1 dc in each st ....(34 sts)
RND 15: 1 dc in next 2 sts, dc2tog, 1 dc in next 15 sts, dc2tog, 1 dc in next 13 sts ....(32 sts)
RND 16: 1 dc in next 3 sts, dc2tog, then (1 dc in next 6 sts, dc2tog) 3 times, 1 dc in next 3 sts ....(28 sts)
RND 17: 1 dc in each st..............(28 sts)
RND 18: (1 dc in next 5 sts, dc2tog) 4 times............................(24 sts)
RND 19: 1 dc in each st, sl st......(24 sts)
Finish off, leaving long tail.
Stuff firmly.

DISPLAY ON THE BODY
Crochet in rows. At the end of each row, ch 1 and turn.
Using col 3, ch 10.
Row 1: 1 dc in 2nd ch from hook, 1 dc in next 8 chs ....(9 sts)
Rows 2-7: 1 dc in each st ....(9 sts)
Row 8: 2 dc in next st, 1 dc in next 8 sts, 2 dc in next st............................. (11 sts)
Row 8 will be the top of the display.
Now we will be working along the other 3 sides of the display, as follows:
Work 6 dc along the side of the display.
Along the bottom, work 2 dc into the first st, 1 dc in next 7 sts, 2 dc in last st.
Along the other side, work 6 dc.
To finish, work 1 sl st into 1st st of row 8.
Finish off, leaving long tail. Work 1 fst sl st.

Making the display screen for the body

ARMS
(Make 2)
Using col 1, make magic ring,
RND 1: 6 dc in magic ring............(6 sts)
RND 2: (1 dc in next st, 2 dc in next 2

sts) 2 times ....(10 sts)
RNDS 3-4: 1 dc in each st...........(10 sts)
Change to col 2.
RND 5: 1 dc in each st ....(10 sts)
RND 6: (dc2tog, 1 dc in next 3 sts) 2 times...............................(8 sts)
RNDS 7-17: 1 dc in each st...........(8 sts)
Stuff three-quarters of the arm.
Work 1 dc in next 2 sts, fold arm in half and, through both sides, work 1 dc in next 3 sts, then sl st.
Fasten off, leaving long tail.

Using col 1, embroider two lines on each arm, the first between rows 7-8, and the second between rows 8-9. To do this, embroider a few short lines 2-3 sts wide between the rows. With a needle, wrap the thread 2-3 times around each embroidered short line to connect them into two whole straight lines around the arm.
Finish off and weave in ends.

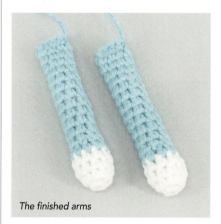

The finished arms

LEGS
(Make 2)
Using col 2, make magic ring.
RND 1: 7 dc in magic ring............(7 sts)
RND 2: 2 dc in each st .... (14 sts)
RND 3: (1 dc in next st, 2 dc in next st) 7 times............................(21 sts)
RND 4: In BLO, 1 dc in each st......(21 sts)
RND 5: (1 dc in next 5 sts, dc2tog) 3 times...........................(18 sts)
RND 6: 1 dc in each st ....(18 sts)
RND 7: dc2tog, 1 dc in next 3 sts, dc2tog 5 times, 1 dc in next 3 sts ....
....(12 sts)
RNDS 8 to 11: 1 dc in each st ..... (12 sts)
RND 12: 1 dc in next 2 sts, dc2tog, 1 dc in next 4 sts, dc2tog, 1 dc in next 2 sts. (10 sts)
RNDS 13 to 16: 1 dc in each st. (10 sts)

Work 5-7 more dc so the last stitch will be directly at the left side of the leg when the front is facing forwards. The front of the leg is where you made the 5 dc2tog in rnd 7.

Fold the leg in half and, working through both sides, work 1 dc in next 4 sts, sl st.

Finish off, leaving long tail.

Using col 1, crochet around lower edge of the leg with sl st through the left free loops between rnds 3 and 4.

Turn the leg so the lower part is facing you. Insert the hook into the last free loop, pull up a loop, insert the hook into the next free loop, work first sl st, then work 20 more sl st in the next free loops along the rnd.

Finish off, work 1 fst sl st, weave in ends.

How your leg stripes should look

Attach head to body

The leg

LINES ON THE LEGS

Embroider two lines on each leg as you did for the arms. Embroider the first line between rnds 6 and 7, and the second between rnds 7 and 8 using col 1.

At first embroider a few short lines 3-4 stitches wide, then, with a help of a needle, wrap the thread 3-4 times around each embroidered short line to connect them in two whole straight lines around each leg.

Finish off and weave in ends.

ASSEMBLY

1 Attach the body to the head with pins between rnds 25 and 26.

2 Sew the body to the head using the left free loops on the head as shown. Stuff firmly as you go. Weave in ends. ⇨

Pin the arms in place before sewing

ARMS

Attach the arms to the body with pins between rnds 18 and 19. When you're sure they're symmetrical, sew and weave in ends.

LEGS

1 Attach the legs to the body with pins between rnds 1 and 2, closer to the front of the body with 2-3 stitches separating them. Sew the legs to the body and weave in ends.

2 Attach the display to the body with pins between rnds 5 and 15. Sew display to the body and weave in ends. Do not stuff.

3 Embroider graphics, lines and buttons on the display using thin coloured threads. Or, if preferred make a rainbow using the following instructions:

RAINBOW

You will be working in rows. At the end of each row, ch 1 and turn your work. Leave enough of a tail at the beginning of your work to attach it to the display. Using col 4, ch 6.
Row 1: 2 dc in 2nd ch from hook, then (1 dc in next ch, 2 dc in next ch) 2 times (8

Leg placement

sts)
Change to col 5.
Row 2: (2 dc in next st, 1 dc in next st) 4 times.. (12 sts)
Change to col 6.
Row 3: (2 dc in next st, 1 dc in next 2 sts) 4 times .... (16 sts)
Ch 1 and fasten off, leaving a long tail for sewing.
Weave in the coloured ends that won't be used for attaching to the robot. Attach the rainbow to the display with pins, then use the tails of cols 4 and 6 to sew. Do not stuff.
Weave in ends.

Sew on body screen

Embroided graphics, lines and buttons

Pattern by:

Svetla Art

Svetla creates crochet toys that help develop children's creative skills, logical thinking, and hand-eye coordination.

www.etsy.com/shop/
SvetlaArtCrochet

You Will Need...

Yarn:
■ You will need to use 4 ply weight cotton yarn in your chosen colours. We have used:
■ Colour 1: Red (100yds)
■ Colour 2: Orange (100yds)
■ Colour 3: Yellow (100yds)
■ Colour 4: Green (150yds)
■ Colour 5: Light Blue (200yds)
■ Colour 6: Dark Blue
■ Colour 7: Purple (100yds)
■ Colour 8: White
■ Colour 9: Black

Tools:
■ 2mm hook
■ Scissors
■ Yarn needle

Other:
■ Fibrefill stuffing

Pattern

Finished product sizes:
Pyramid: 13cm/5in tall
Sphere: 8cm/3in diameter
Cylinder: 11.5cm/4.5in high,
5cm (1.9in) wide
Prism: 8cm/3in high, 9.5cm/3.5in wide
Cube: 7cm/2.9in tall, 7cm/2.9in wide
Cuboid: 11cm/4.3in tall, 6.5cm/2.5in wide
Cone: 7cm/2.8in high, 7cm/3.5in diameter

COLOURFUL SHAPES

HELP YOUR LITTLE ONES LEARN THEIR SHAPES WITH THESE CUTE CHARACTERS

EYES
(Make 14)
Using col 8, make a magic ring.
RND 1: 6 dc in magic ring.............. (6sts)
RND 2: 2 dc in each st ....(12sts)
Fasten off, and weave in loose ends.

Cut the yarn and leave a long tail for sewing. Use col 9 to embroider the pupil.

PYRAMID
SIDES
(Make 3)
Using col 1, ch 16.
ROW 1: 1 dc in 2nd chain from hook, 1 dc in each st ....(15 sts)
ROWS 2-4: ch 1, turn,
1 dc in each st ....(15 sts)
ROW 5: dc2tog, 1 dc in next 11 sts, dc2tog...(13 sts)
ROWS 6-8: 1 dc in each st...........(13 sts)
ROW 9: dc2tog, 1 dc in next 9 sts, dc2tog...(11 sts)
ROWS 10-12: 1 dc in each st ....(11 sts)
ROW 13: dc2tog, 1 dc in next 7 sts, dc2tog.. (9 sts)
ROWS 14-16: 1 dc in each st .... (9 sts)
ROW 17: dc2tog, 1 dc in next 5 sts, dc2tog.. (7 sts)
ROWS 18-20: 1 dc in each st........ (7 sts)
ROW 21: dc2tog, 1 dc in next 3 sts, dc2tog.. (5 sts)
ROWS 22-24: 1 dc in each st. (5 sts)
ROW 25: dc2tog, 1 dc in next st, dc2tog .... (3 sts)
ROWS 26-28: 1 dc in each st........ (3 sts)
ROW 29: dc2tog, 1 dc
in next st.................................... (2 sts)
ROW 30: dc2tog........................... (1 st)
Finish off, leaving long tail for assembly.

On one side, sew the eyes and embroider

the mouth, eyebrows with black thread.

Line up the diagonal sides of 2 of the triangles and crochet them together using dc.

Attach the 3rd triangle to the remaining sides using dc.

Stuff the cone with fibrefill, keeping the shape.

BOTTOM
Using col 1, ch 16.
ROW 1: 1 dc in 2nd chain from hook, 1 dc in each st................................(15 sts)
ROW 2: 1 dc in each st...............(15 sts)
ROW 3: dc2tog, 1 dc in next 11 sts,, dc2tog ....(13 sts)
ROW 4: 1 dc each st...................(13 sts)
ROW 5: dc2tog, 1 dc in next 9 sts, dctog ....(11 sts)
ROW 6: 1 dc in each st...............(11 sts)

ROW 7: dc2tog, 1 dc in next 7 sts,
dc2tog .... (9 sts)
ROW 8: 1 dc in each st .... (9 sts)
ROW 9: dc2tog, 1 dc in next 5 sts,
dc2tog .... (7 sts)
ROW 10: 1 dc in each st .... (7 sts)
ROW 11: dc2tog, 1 dc in next 3 sts,
dc2tog .... (5 sts)
ROW 12: 1 dc in each st. .... (5 sts)
ROW 13: dc2tog, 1 dc in next st,
dc2tog .... (3 sts)
ROW 14: 1 dc in each st .... (3 sts)
ROW 15: dc3tog .... (1 st)
Attach to the bottom of all three sides using
dc.

Finish off and weave in ends.

SPHERE

The sphere is made in spiral rounds - they
are not connected by a slip stitch at the end
of each round.
Using col 2, make a magic ring.
RND 1: 6 dc in magic ring .... (6 sts)
RND 2: 2 dc in each st .... (12 sts)
RND 3: (1 dc in next st, 2 dc in next st) 6
times ....(18 sts)
RND 4: (1 dc in next 2 sts, 2 dc in next
st) 6 times .... (24 sts)
RND 5: (1 dc in next 3 sts, 2 dc in next
st) 6 times .... (30 sts)
RND 6: (1 dc in next 4 sts, 2 dc in next
st) 6 times .... (36 sts)
RND 7: (1 dc in next 5 sts, 2 dc in next
st) 6 times .... (42 sts)
RND 8: (1 dc in next 6 sts, 2 dc in next
st) 6 times .... (48 sts)

RND 9: (1 dc in next 7 sts, 2 dc in next
st) 6 times .... (54 sts)
RNDS 10-16: 1 dc in each st .... (54 sts)
RND 17: (1 dc in next 7 sts, dc2tog) 6
times .... (48 sts)
RND 18: (1 dc in next 7 sts, dc2tog) 6
times .... (42 sts)
RND 19: (1 dc in next 5 sts, dc2tog) 6
times .... (36 sts)
Sew on the eyes and embroider the mouth,
eyebrows with black thread.

Begin stuffing.

RND 20: (1 dc in next 4 sts, dc2tog) 6
times .... (30 sts)
RND 21: (1 dc in next 3 sts, dc2tog) 6
times .... (24 sts)
RND 22: (1 dc in next 2 sts, dc2tog) 6
times ....(18 sts)
RND 23: (1 dc in next st, dc2tog) 6
times ....(12 sts)
Add more stuffing.
RND 24: dc2tog 6 times .... (6 sts)
Finish off, leaving a long tail. Using a yarn
needle, weave the tail to tighten the hole.

Cut yarn and weave in ends.

Crochet TOYBOX

CYLINDER

Using col 3, ch 26.
ROW 1: 1 dc in 2nd chain from hook, 1 dc in each st .... (25 sts)
ROWS 2-30: ch 1, turn, 1 dc in each st. . (25 sts)
Sew on the eyes and embroider the mouth and eyebrows with black thread.

Fold the rectangle and sew the long sides together with the yarn needle.

TOP

Using col 3, make magic ring.
RND 1: 6 dc in magic ring............. (6 sts)
RND 2: 2 dc in each st ....(12 sts)
RND 3: (1 dc in next st, 2 dc in next st) 6 times...(18 sts)
RND 4: (1 dc in next 2 sts, 2 dc in next st) 6 times.................................. (24 sts)
RND 5: (1 dc in next 3 sts, 2 dc in next st) 6 times.................................. (30 sts)
Attach top to the cylinder using dc.

Finish off and weave in ends.

BOTTOM

Using col 3, make magic ring.
RND 1: 6 dc in magic ring............. (6 sts)
RND 2: 2 dc in each st ....(12 sts)

RND 3: (1 dc in next st, 2 dc in next st) 6 times...(18 sts)
RND 4: (1 dc in next 2 sts, 2 dc in next st) 6 times................................. (24 sts)
RND 5: (1 dc in next 3 sts, 2 dc in next st) 6 times.................................. (30 sts)
Attach bottom to cylinder using dc, adding stuffing as you go to keep the cylinder's shape.

PRISM
FRONT AND BACK

(Make 2)
Using col 4, ch 21.
ROW 1: 1 dc in 2nd ch from hook, 1 dc in each st .... (20 sts)
ROW 2: 1 dc in each st .... (20 sts)
ROW 3: dc2tog, 1 dc in next 16 sts, dc2tog...(18 sts)
ROWS 4-6: 1 dc in each st...........(18 sts)
ROW 7: dc2tog, 1 dc in next 14 sts, dc2tog...(16 sts)
ROWS 8-10: 1 dc in each st ....(16 sts)
ROW 11: dc2tog, 1 dc in next 12 sts, dc2tog...(14 sts)
ROWS 12-15: 1 dc in each st........(14 sts)
ROW 16: dc2tog, 1 dc in next 10 sts, dc2tog...(12 sts)
ROWS 17-18: 1 dc in each st........(12 sts)
Finish off leaving tail for sewing.

SIDES

(Make 2)
Using col 4, ch 13.
ROW 1: 1 dc in 2nd ch from hook, 1 dc in each st ....(12 sts)
ROWS 2-18: 1 dc in each st ....(12 sts)

Attach the sides to the diagonals on the front and back using dc. Finish off.

Sew on the eyes to the front, and embroider the mouth and eyebrows with black thread.

TOP

Using col 4, ch 13.
ROW 1: 1 dc in 2nd ch from hook, 1 dc in each ch ....(12 sts)
ROWS 2-12: 1 dc in each st ....(12 sts)
Attach the top on all 4 sides using dc. Finish off and weave in ends.

Start stuffing using fibrefill.

BOTTOM

Using col 4, ch 23.
ROW 1: 1 dc in 2nd ch from hook, 1 dc in each ch .... (22 sts)
ROWS 2-12: 1 dc in each st............. (22 sts)

Use the faces to add some personality

How to sew together your prism

How your cube will look before attaching ends

Attach the bottom on all 4 sides using dc. Finish stuffing as you go.

Finish off and weave in ends.

CUBE
SIDES
(Make 6)
Using col 5, ch 16.
ROW 1: 1 dc in 2nd ch from hook, 1 dc each ch. (15 sts)

ROWS 2-15: 1 dc in each st. (15 sts) Finish off.

ASSEMBLY
Sew on the eyes to one of the sides, and embroider the mouth and eyebrows with black thread.

Take 2 pieces and attach them along one side using dc. Repeat with another 2 sides to create a cube tube.

Attach other 2 sides using dc, stuffing as you go. Weave in ends.

CUBOID
SIDES
(Make 4)
Using col 6, ch 26.
ROW 1: 1 dc in 2nd ch from hook, 1 dc in each ch ....(25 sts)
ROWS 2-15: 1 dc in each st..............(25 sts)

Finish off.

On 1 side, attach eyes, and embroider mouth and eyebrows with black yarn.

Take 2 sides and attach them along one long side using dc. Repeat with the remaining sides to create a rectangular tube.

ENDS
(Make 2)
Using col 6, ch 16.
ROW 1: 1 dc in 2nd ch from hook, 1 dc in each ch ....(15 sts)
ROWS 2-15: 1 dc in each st................(15 sts)
Attach 1 end using dc along all 4 sides.

Stuff firmly, keeping the shape of the cuboid.

Attach other end using dc along all 4 sides.

Weave in ends.

CONE
BASE
Using col 7, make magic ring.
RND 1: 6 dc in magic ring....................(6 sts)
RND 2: 2 dc in each st........................(12 sts)

RND 3: (1 dc in next st, 2 dc in next st) 6 times...(18 sts)
RND 4: (1 dc in next 2 sts, 2 dc in next st) 6 times...(24 sts)
RND 5: (1 dc in next 3 sts, 2 dc in next st) 6 times... (30 sts)
RND 6: (1 dc in next 4 sts, 2 dc in next st) 6 times...(36 sts)
RND 7: (1 dc in next 5 sts, 2 dc in next st) 6 times...(42 sts)
RND 8: (1 dc in next 6 sts, 2 dc in next st) 6 times...(48 sts)
RND 9: (1 dc in next 7 sts, 2 dc in next st) 6 times... (54 sts)
Finish off.

CONE
Using col 7, make magic ring.
RND 1: 6 dc in magic ring....................(6 sts)
RND 2: (1 dc in next st, 2 dc in next st) 3 times...(9 sts)
RND 3: (1 dc in next 2 sts, 2 dc in next st) 3 times...(12 sts)
RND 4: (1 dc in next 3 sts, 2 dc in next st) 3 times...(15 sts)
RND 5: (1 dc in next 4 sts, 2 dc in next st) 3 times...(18 sts)
RND 6: (1 dc in next 5 sts, 2 dc in next st) 3 times...(21 sts)
RND 7: (1 dc in next 6 sts, 2 dc in next st) 3

times..(24 sts)
RND 8: (1 dc in next 7 sts, 2 dc in next st) 3 times...(27 sts)
RND 9: (1 dc in next 8 sts, 2 dc in next st) 3 times... (30 sts)
RND 10: (1 dc in next 9 sts, 2 dc in next st) 3 times...(33 sts)
RND 11: (1 dc in next 10 sts, 2 dc in next st) 3 times...(36 sts)
RND 12: (1 dc in next 11 sts, 2 dc in next st) 3 times...(39 sts)
RND 13: (1 dc in next 12 sts, 2 dc in next st) 3 times...(42 sts)
RND 14: (1 dc in next 13 sts, 2 dc in next st) 3 times...(45 sts)
RND 15: (1 dc in next 14 sts, 2 dc in next st) 3 times...(48 sts)
RND 16: (1 dc in next 15 sts, 2 dc in next st) 3 times...(51 sts)
RND 17: (1 dc in next 16 sts, 2 dc in next st) 3 times... (54 sts)
Sew the eyes onto the cone and embroider mouth and eyebrows.

Attach base to cone using dc, stuffing as you to keep the cone's shape.

Finish off and weave in ends.

"Sew the eyes onto the cone and embroider the mouth and eyebrows"

How to stitch your cone together

LITTLE CHICK BEAN BAG

Pattern by:

Kara Gunza

Kara's grandmother taught her how to crochet when she was about 10 years old and it sparked a love of stitching and fibre work that continues today more than 30 years later! On her blog, Petals to Picots, she shares my passion for crochet, as well as knitting, needle felting, and other fibre crafts.

www.petalstopicots.com

You Will Need...

Yarn:
- You will need to use aran weight cotton yarn in your chosen colours. Here we have used Lion Brand 24/7 Cotton in:
- Colour 1: Tangerine
- Colour 2: Ecru
- Colour 3: Red
- Colour 4: Lemon
- A small amount of black yarn

Tools:
- 5mm hook (US H/8)
- 4mm hook (US G/6)
- Yarn needle
- Scissors

Other:
- Fibrefill stuffing

Optional:
- Dried beans

A PERFECT TOY FOR ANY CHILD WHO LOVES FARMYARD ANIMALS

Pattern

Finished product size: Finished chick size: approx 7.6cm/3½ in
Finished mama size: approx 7.6cm/3½ in

* NOTE: The pattern is written for both the chick and the mama, with a / separating the stitch counts. For instance ch 13/17 means to chain 13 for the chick and 17 for the mama. The same is also true for the stitch counts at the end of rows.

BODY
With a 5mm hook and col 2/1, ch 13/17.
ROW 1: 1 dc in 2nd ch from hook and each ch across, turn. (12/16 sts)
ROW 2: ch 1 (does not count as st), 1 dc in each st across, turn. (12/16 sts)
ROWS 3-28/38: Repeat Row 2.
Fold the piece so that row 1 lines up with the last row, slip stitch together to the corner, then slip stitch down side to fold. Place a marker at fold on open edge
Fasten off and weave in ends.

FACE DETAIL
Use 4mm hook for Baby and 5mm hook for Mama.
Join col 3 in 4th st from slip stitched corner, ch 3 (counts as tr), work 2 tr in same st as join, 1 dc in next, 3 tr in next,

1 dc in next, 3 htr in next, 1 dc in next, sl st in next, fasten off.

Join colour 4 in next st, ch 1, work 1 dc in the same st as join, ch 3, 1 dc in furthest ch from hook, 1 dc in next st, sl st in same st, fasten off.

Skip next st, join col 3 in next st, ch 1, 1 htr in same st as join, ch 1, sl st in same st, fasten off.

Weave in ends.

With black, make a french knot for each eye as shown.

Filled with beans

Turn the piece so the opening is in the back. Stuff a little fibrefill stuffing into the head. Fill about 3/4 of the way with dried beans. Close pouch matching marker on fold to top seam and sl st closed.

GAMES

Pattern by:

Kara Gunza

Kara's grandmother taught her how to crochet when she was about 10 years old and it sparked a love of stitching and fibre work that continues today more than 30 years later! On her blog, Petals to Picots, she share her passion for crochet, as well as knitting, needle felting, and other fibre crafts.

www.petalstopicots.com

You Will Need...

Yarn:
- Worsted weight yarn in your chosen colours. Here we have used Lion Brand Vanna's Choice in:
- White (approx. 300-450 yd)
- Scarlet (approx. 156 yd)
- Charcoal grey (approx. 156 yd)
- Small amount of black

Tools:
- 5mm hook (US H-8) or smaller depending on your tension (see notes)
- Yarn needle
- Stitch markers

Other:
- Fibrefill stuffing

Optional:
- Bean bags (see notes)

TEN-PIN BOWLING SET

BRING THE BOWLING ALLEY TO YOUR LIVING ROOM WITH THIS FUN SET

Use whatever hook size allows you to achieve a nice tight fabric. The tighter the gauge, the better the shape and structure of each piece will be.
You can use bean bags in the base of each pin and in the center of the ball to add a little weight. To make your own, use uncooked rice or dried beans and place between two squares of fabric. Sew closed at each side, making sure the contents cannot come out. Filling an old sock (with no holes, of course) works great too!
Please note that as with all items given to small children, this crochet bowling set should be checked regularly for pulls or unraveling stitches that may allow stuffing to come out and become a choking hazard.
As always, infants and small children should be supervised.

Pattern

Finished pin size: approximately 34cm/9½in high and 25.5cm/10 in around
Finished bowling ball size: approximately 45cm/18in around

BOWLING PIN

Make 6 pins for a fun kid set or 10 for a standard bowling set.
This pattern is worked in separate rounds. At the end of each rnd, sl st to 1st st to join.
At the start of each rnd, 1st st in same st as join.
With white, make a magic ring.
Rnd 1: ch 1 (does not count as st here and throughout), work 6 dc into ring, sl st to join (6 sts)
RND 2: ch 1, 2 dc in each st, sl st to join ....(12 sts)
RND 3: ch 1, 1 dc in each st, sl st to join ....(12 sts)
RND 4: ch 1, (2 dc in next st, 1 dc in next st) around, sl st to join............................(18 sts)

RND 5: ch 1, 1 dc in each st, sl st to join. ....(18 sts)
RND 6: ch 1, (2 dc in next st, 1 dc in next 2 sts) around, sl st to join......................(24 sts)
RNDS 7-10: ch 1, 1 dc in each st, sl st to join ....(24 sts)
RND 11: ch 1, (dc2tog, 1 dc in next 2 sts), sl st to join...(18 sts)

Change to red yarn.
RND 12: ch 1, 1 dc in each st, sl st to join ....(18 sts)

RND 13: ch 1, (dc2tog, 1 dc in next st) around, sl st to join..............................(12 sts)

Change to white yarn.
RNDS 14-15: ch 1, 1 dc in each st, sl st to join ....(12 sts)

Change to red yarn.

RND 16: ch 1, 1 dc in each st, sl st to join. .. (12 sts)

RND 17: ch 1, (2 dc in next st, 1 dc in next st) around, sl st to join..........................(18 sts)

Change to white yarn.

RND 18: ch 1, 1 dc in each st, sl st to join. .. (18 sts)

RND 19: ch 1, (2 dc in next st, 1 dc in next 2 sts) around, sl st to join.......................(24 sts)

Stuff tip of pin, taking care not to overfill it.

RND 20: ch 1, 1 dc in each st, sl st to join. .. (24 sts)

RND 21: ch 1, (2 dc in next st, 1 dc in next 3 sts) around, sl st to join....................... (30 sts)

RNDS 22-31: ch 1, 1 dc in each st, sl st to join .... (30 sts)

RND 32: ch 1, (dc2tog, 1 dc in next 3 sts) around, sl st to join.............................(24 sts)

RNDS 33-35: ch 1, 1 dc each st, sl st to join (24 sts)

RND 36: ch 1, 1 dc in each st, sl st to join. .. (24 sts)

RND 37: ch 1, working in BLO, (dc2tog, 1 dc in next 2 sts) around, sl st to join.............. ....(18 sts)

Stuff rest of pin, taking care not to over stuff. If using a bean bag, place in last so it is at base of pin.

RND 38: ch 1, (dc2tog, 1 dc in next st) around, sl st to join.............................(12 sts)

RND 39: ch 1, dc2tog around, sl st to join(6 sts)

Fasten off and leave a long tail. Using a yarn needle, weave the tail through each stitch and pull gently to tighten. Weave in ends.

BOWLING BALL

This pattern is worked in separate rounds. At the end of each rnd, sl st to 1st st to join.

At the start of each rnd, 1st st in same st as join.

With grey yarn, make a magic ring.

RND 1: ch 1, work 6 dc into ring, sl st to join (6 sts)

RND 2: ch 1, 2 dc in each st, sl st to join. ....(12 sts)

RND 3: ch 1, (2 dc in next st, 1 dc in next st) around, sl st to join.............................(18 sts)

RND 4: ch 1, (2 dc in next st, 1 dc in next 2 sts) around, sl st to join.......................(24 sts)

RND 5: ch 1, (2 dc in next st, 1 dc in next 3 sts) around, sl st to join....................... (30 sts)

RND 6: ch 1, (2 dc in next st, 1 dc in next 4 sts) around, sl st to join.......................(36 sts)

RND 7: ch 1, (2 dc in next st, 1 dc in next 5 sts) around, sl st to join.......................(42 sts)

RND 8: ch 1, (2 dc in next st, 1 dc in next 6 sts) around, sl st to join.......................(48 sts)

RND 9: ch 1, (2 dc in next st, 1 dc in next 7 sts) around, sl st to join....................... (54 sts)

RND 10: ch 1, (2 dc in next st, 1 dc in next 8 sts) around, sl st to join.......................(60 sts)

RNDS 11-20: ch 1, 1 dc in each st, sl st to join ....(60 sts)

RND 21: ch 1, (dc2tog, 1 dc in next 8 sts) around, sl st to join............................. 54 sts)

RND 22: ch 1, (dc2tog, 1 dc in next 7 sts) around, sl st to join.............................(48 sts)

RND 23: ch 1, (dc2tog, 1 dc in next 6 sts) around, sl st to join.............................(42 sts)

RND 24: ch 1, (dc2tog, 1 dc in next 5 sts) around, sl st to join.............................(36 sts)

RND 25: ch 1, (dc2tog, 1 dc in next 4 sts) around, sl st to join............................. 30 sts)

RND 26: ch 1, (dc2tog, 1 dc in next 3 sts) around, sl st to join.............................(24 sts)

Stuff ball, taking care not to over stuff. If using a bean bag, position it in the centre of the ball.

RND 27: ch 1, (dc2tog, 1 dc in next 2 sts) around, sl st to join.............................(18 sts)

RND 28: ch 1, (dc2tog, 1 dc in next st) around, sl st to join.............................(12 sts)

RND 29: ch 1, dc2tog around, sl st to join(6 sts)

Fasten off and leave a long tail. Using a yarn needle, weave the tail through each stitch and pull gently to tighten. Weave in ends.

FAUX FINGER HOLES
(Make 3)

With black yarn, make a magic ring.

RND 1: ch 1, work 6 dc into ring, join... (6 sts)

Fasten off, leaving a long tail. Using a yarn needle, sew the faux finger holes to the bowling ball. Weave in ends.

NAUGHTS & CROSSES

MAKE YOUR OWN VERSION OF THE CLASSIC
GAME OUT OF GRANNY SQUARES

Tip
The board doubles
as a handy bag to
stow away the
playing pieces.

Pattern

- - - - - - - - - - - -

Board bag measures: 24 x 26cm/9½ x 10¼in

★ **TENSION:** One square measures 8 x 8cm, using 4mm hook.

★ **NOTE:** Yarn amounts are based on average requirements and are therefore approximate. Instructions in square brackets are worked as stated after 2nd bracket.

You Will Need...

- - - - - - - - - -

Yarn:

- 1 x 100g (295m) ball of Stylecraft Special DK (100% acrylic) in each of these colours:
- Mustard (1823)
- Aster (1003)
- Magenta (1084)
- Kelly Green (1826)

Tools:

- 4mm hook (US G/6)
- Tweezers

Other:

- Toy stuffing

BOARD BAG

First side: Square (make 9)

RND 1: With 4mm hook, wind Mustard round index finger of left hand to form a slip ring, insert hook into ring, yarn round hook and pull through, ch 3 (counts as 1 tr), 15 tr into ring, slst in top of 3ch, pull end tightly to close ring.......(16 sts)

RND2: ch 3 (counts as 1 tr), work 1 tr, 2 ch and 2 tr all in base of 3ch, 1 htr in next st, 1 dc in next st, 1 htr in next st, (work 2 tr, 2ch and 2 tr all in next st, 1 htr in next st, 1 dc in next st, 1 htr in next st) 3 times, slst in top of 3ch.

RND 3: ch 3 (counts as 1 tr), 1 tr in next st, work 2 tr, 2 ch and 2 tr all in chsp, (1 tr in each of next 7 sts, work 2 tr, 2 ch and 2 tr in next chsp) 3 times, 1 tr in each of last 5 sts, slst in top of 3ch ... (44 sts)

RND 4: ch 3 (counts as 1 tr), 1 tr in each of next 3 sts, work 2 tr, 2 ch and 2 tr all in chsp, (1 tr in each of next 11 sts, work 2 tr, 2 ch and 2 tr all in next chsp) 3 times, 1 tr in each of last 7 sts, slst in top of 3ch.....................................(60 sts)

Fasten off.

Arrange squares in 3 rows of 3 squares each and join squares horizontally as follows: With wrong side of two squares together and using 4mm hook, join Aster to corner chsp of both squares, ch 1, insert hook under both strands of final round on each square and work 1 dc, continue working dc along edge to next corner, then work dc along next two pair of squares.

Fasten off.

Work another horizontal join in same way, then join squares vertically as before.

Second side: Using Aster instead of Mustard and Mustard instead of Aster, work as first side.

With 4m hook and using Magenta, join sides together along three edges in same way as squares, working 3 dc in each corner chsp.

Opening edging: With right side facing and using 4m hook, join Magenta to top of seam at open end of one side, ch 1, 1 dc in same place as join, work 53 dc evenly along edge to next seam, 1 dc in seam, then work 53 dc along other side, slst in first dc. ....(108 sts)

Next round: ch 3 (counts as 1 dtr), 1dtr in each st, slst in top of 3ch.

Next round: ch 1, 1 dc in each st, slst in 1ch. Fasten off.

Cord: With 4m hook and Kelly Green, ch 125.

RND 1: 1 dc in 2nd ch from hook, 1 dc in each ch, slst in side of last dc and ch, now work along other side of ch thus: ch 1, 1 dc in each ch to end. Fasten off.

Thread cord between dtr of opening edging, taking cord over 6 dtr each time. Join short ends of cord.

NOUGHTS

(Make 5)

RND 1: With 4mm hook, wind Kelly Green round index finger of left hand to form a slip ring, insert hook into ring, yarn round hook and pull through, 1ch (does not count as a st), 9dc into ring, pull end tightly to close ring.

RNDS 2-35: 1 dc in each st.

Fasten off.

Using tweezers, stuff firmly.

Join fastened off edge to top of first round.

CROSSES

(Make 5)

Whole bar: RND 1: With 4mm hook, wind Magenta round index finger of left hand to form a slip ring, insert hook into ring, yarn round hook and pull through, ch 1 (does not count as a st), 6 dc into ring, pull end tightly to close ring.

RND 2: (2 dc in next st, 1 dc in next st) 3 times..(9 sts)

RNDS 3-15: 1 dc in each st ....(9 sts)

Using tweezers, stuff firmly.

RND 16: (dc2tog, 1 dc in next st) 3 times (6 sts)

RND 17: dc2tog 3 times ....(3 sts)

Fasten off.

Run end along top of last round, pull up tightly and secure.

HALF BARS

(Make 2)

RND 1: With 4mm hook, wind Magenta round index finger of left hand to form a slip ring, insert hook into ring, yarn round hook and pull through, ch 1 (does not count as a st), 6 dc into ring, pull end tightly to close ring.

RND 2: (2 dc in next st, 1 dc in next st) 3 times... (9 sts)

RNDS 3-6: 1 dc in each st...........(9 sts)

Fasten off.

Using tweezers, stuff firmly.

Sew open end of one half bar to centre of whole bar, then sew other half at opposite side.

AMISH PUZZLE BALL

KEEP LITTLE HANDS OCCUPIED WITH THIS TOY THAT'S GREAT FOR FIDGETERS

Pattern by:

Dedri Uys

Passionate about crochet, Dedri spends as much time as she can crocheting. Her book, Amamani Puzzle Balls, is available to buy on Amazon, and she's known in the crochet community for creating Sophie's Universe..

www.lookatwhatimade.net

You Will Need...

Yarn:
- You will need to use 4 ply yarn. Here we have used Scheepjes Stonewashed in:
- Colour 1: Smokey Quartz (842) (2 balls)
- Colour 2: Turquoise (864) (1 ball)
- Colour 3: Beryl (873) (1 ball)
- Scheepjes Riverwashed in:
- Colour 4: Amazon (991) (1 ball)

Tools:
- 4.5mm hook (US G/7)
- Scissors
- Yarn needle

Other:
- Fibrefill stuffing

Optional:
- Squeakers, bells, rattles, buttons, beads etc to put inside the toy

Pattern

- - - - - - - - - - - -

Finished product size: 15cm/6in in diameter

★ **GAUGE:** It is important that you work as tight as you can so that your stuffing doesn't show through.

★ **NOTES:** Ensure that you stuff the segments very well (more than you think you need to).

★ If you find you're crocheting too loose, try going down a hook size or two to create tighter stitches.

WEDGES

(Make 12)

These wedges are worked in rows and joined with a seam.

ROW 1: using col 1, ch 2, 3 dc in 2nd ch from hook, turn .... (3 sts)

ROW 2: ch 1, 2 dc in each st, turn ..... (6 sts)

ROW 3: ch 1, (2 dc in next st, 1 dc in next st) 3 times, turn .... (9 sts)

ROW 4: ch 1, (2 dc in next st, 1 dc in next 2 sts) 3 times, turn ....(12 sts)

ROW 5: ch 1, (2 dc in next st, 1 dc in next 3 sts) 3 times, turn ....(15 sts)

ROW 6: ch 1, (2 dc in next st, 1 dc in next 4 sts) 3 times, turn ....(18 sts)

ROW 7: ch 1, (2 dc in next st, 1 dc in next 5 sts) 3 times, tur.................. (21 sts)

ROW 8: ch 1, (2 dc in next st, 1 dc in next 6 sts) 3 times, turn .... (24 sts)

ROW 9: ch 1, (2 dc in next st, 1 dc in ⟹

Crochet TOYBOX

next 7 sts) 3 times, turn .... (27 sts)
ROW 10: ch 1, (2 dc in next st, 1 dc in next 8 sts) 3 times, ch 1, **do not turn** .... (30 sts)
Fold the half-circle in half so that the end containing the hook is closest to you (see top photo). Insert your hook into the first row down the side of the resulting wedge (through both layers – see photo above) and make a dc. Make 8 more dc, working into each row down the side and through both layers. Remember to put your initial yarn end inside the wedge before closing it completely. When you get to the end, ch 1 and fasten off (see three photos at top of page).
To get rid of the final yarn end, insert your hook into one of the stitches at the pointy end of the wedge (from the inside of the wedge to the outside) and pull the end through to the inside of the wedge.
If you want to, you can turn the resulting wedge inside out so that you don't end up with a seam.

CHAIN OF 'LIDS'
(Make 3)
Make one each in cols 2, 3 and 4.
ROW 1: ch 2, 2 dc in 2nd ch from hook, turn .... (2 sts)
ROW 2: ch 1, 1 dc in each st, turn..(2 sts)
ROW 3: ch 1, 2 dc in each st, turn..... (4 sts)
ROW 4: ch 1, 1 dc in each st, turn.......(4 sts)
ROW 5: ch 1, 2 dc in the first st, 1 dc in next 2 sts, 2 dc in next st, turn ....
.... (6 sts)
ROWS 6-9: ch 1, 1 dc in each st, turn. ... (6 sts)
ROW 10: ch 1, dc2tog, 1 dc in next 2 sts, dc2tog, turn............................ (4 sts)
ROW 11: ch 1, 1 dc in each st, turn.......(4 sts)
ROW 12: ch 1, dc2tog twice, turn..... (2 sts)
ROW 13: ch 1, dc in each st, turn....... (2 sts)
ROW 14: ch 1, dc2tog, don't fasten off(1

st)
Repeat rows 1-14 three more times. This will give you a chain of 4 'lids'.

On the very last lid of the chain, ch 1 and fasten off.

ASSEMBLY
1 You will be attaching 4 wedges to each chain of lids, working up the chain of lids on one side and then down the other side, stuffing as you go. You will be working into each st of the wedge opening and each row of the chain of lids.

2 With a col 1 slip knot already on your hook, place your first wedge behind the first lid on the right (with the dc seam of the wedge to your right – see Photo 1) and insert your hook through the first st of the chain of lids and the first st of the opening of one of the wedges (Photo 2). Make a dc through both layers. Make 14 more dc, working into each row of the lid and each stitch of the wedge.

3 Join the next wedge to its lid in the same way (Photo 3) and continue until you have attached one side of each of the 4 wedges and lids.

④ Now you will be closing the wedges. Insert your hook into the same (last) st of the 4th lid and the next st of the 4th wedge and make a dc. Continue working through both layers as before, making 15 dc along the other side of each wedge and lid (Photo 4), stuffing as you go.

⑤ When you reach the last st of the first wedge, join to the first st with a sl st and fasten off, leaving a 10cm/4in end. Use the end to sew the tips of the first and last wedges together thoroughly. You have now completed one segment. Repeat for the remaining two segments.

BUILDING YOUR AMISH PUZZLE BALL

Ⓐ When your segments are all nicely stuffed and neatly finished off, slip one segment over the other segment so that they form a cross.

Ⓑ Slip the third segment over both of the other segments, slotting the wedges into the holes around the side of the cross.